M000306205

About the Book

I never wanted a dog. I received one as a gift from my son and daughter. Through my experiences with Kona, I discovered the real meaning of life and rediscovered God's awesome presence and unconditional love.

KONA'S TALE

A DIFFERENT KIND OF LOVE STORY

BY JOE DEMARTINO

Copyright © 2020 Joe DeMartino.

ALL RIGHTS RESERVED. This book contains material protected under International and Federal Copyright Laws and Treaties. Any unauthorized reprint or use of this material is prohibited. No part of this book may be reproduced or transmitted in any form or by any means, electronic or mechanical, including photocopying, recording, or by any information storage and retrieval system without express written permission from the author/publisher.

ISBN: 978-1-64184-396-6 (Paperback)
ISBN: 978-1-64184-397-3 (eBook)

August 2020

Dedication

To God's Angel, my mother, Angela--the most wonderful, humble, simple but powerful and unselfish
woman I have ever known. Through her incredible
courage, loyalty, dedication, discipline, love of Jesus
and Mother Mary, she influenced my life to an
immeasurable degree. I miss you every day!

Acknowledgements

I learned writing a book is harder and requires more endurance than the many marathons I have run. This would not have been possible without my amazing wife Maureen (Mo) who has loved and supported me on the wild adventure we have taken together in this life. Her support and patience were paramount. Thank you!

Special thanks to my son Joey DeMartino, for his selfless commitment in choosing to join the military, becoming a decorated combat veteran in service to our country. To my daughter Jenna DeMartino, an astounding, gifted musician and teacher, for giving me the gift of watching her dream as a five-year old become a reality. Both have inspired me to continue personally growing beyond what they realize.

Thank you to my brother John and sister Jeanne for our childhood together, during what were, to say the least, enduring times. The closeness we share and the level of commitment they have made to their families influenced me tremendously.

To Jim Cipollone, my oldest and dearest friend, a brother really. Thanks for the laughs, the tears, for being there for each other in the best and worst of times. You have been a grounding rod and sounding board on many issues since we were seventeen years old.

To Doug Robinson, who helped validate that real friendship knows no time nor distance. Over the years we built an incredible, deep bond while living 3,000 miles apart. Thank you for being there in the fun and not-so-fun times.

Thank you to Tom Bird, for introducing me to the Divine author within, and for his coaching, putting up with my frustrations and helping me through the process. Thank you also to the entire publishing team and to Donna Velasco, whose quiet and persistent belief in me and the process, was key to my initial and continued engagement.

Thanks to Cat Bendure, for our deep spiritual relationship, her extraordinary connection with non-human animals and for helping me interpret their signals.

Contents

Introduction

Life lessons come in so many ways. In our world of things that seem to matter, have we lost touch with what really does matter? It's not about things, it is about our connection to a higher purpose. To be in touch with our authentic "me." Who is that? Why is that? Where is that? Why won't you show yourself?

Look in the mirror. More importantly, look deeply into your own eyes and say I love you to "me"? How can we be there and give love to others if not there for "me" first? How many are not able to do it?

The greatest fear humanity has is that we are insignificant, we don't really matter much, we're just one of the pack, just another person. We wonder why so many have different life experiences, some good, some bad. Why? God, Spirit are you there, we ask? REALLY, are you there? Why then? Why the hurt and pain on good people?

CHAPTER 1

A Cold Winter's Night

(KONA)

It was a cold winter night in December in 2008 when it all began. Well, that's when it began here on earth, but the real story started a long time ago. Little did Joe or I know we were to be inextricably linked on a mission, a mission for each of us, a mission to help so many others get what they need and deserve.

That night I found myself being packed up and loaded into the machine humans like Joe call a car which went to a place I didn't recognize. I was eight weeks old at the time and confused as to why I was being taken away from my siblings, my pack. I did recall my human pack leader mom talking on the phone the other day and all I could sense was a new home was coming soon.

We can determine a lot by smell and certainly the smells were different that day. I wondered why. What did I do wrong? Was I not worthy? Was I not loved? Would I and it all be okay? Who would take care of me? Why am I here and why do I have to be the one to go?

I was loaded into a dog crate and off I went into this behemoth machine called an airplane. I wasn't alone, there were several of us four-legged canines in the same situation. There was a guy named Charlie, a large 100-pound breed known as a German Shepherd. We made eye contact and did the typical say hello, the way we dogs do; sniff, sniff tails, wag, check each other out. He also seemed apprehensive about where he was going and why. There was another guy named "Whitey," known as an Alaskan Malamute. He was a big boy, broad shoulders and a big chest. He was frantic with energy. We all shared similar levels of uncertainty about the situation.

Interestingly, humans are not the only creatures who experience trepidation, fear, nervousness, and anxiety. Nor are they the only ones that want and need to be loved and cared for, wanting and needing to have a purpose, learning how to compete in a complex environment. We dogs do as well. More about that later.

Finally, we get some food and water, get loaded into the crates. Wow, I don't recognize many smells here. No doubt lots of other canines were here before me. I don't like this place very much. They load us into the belly of this metallic beast, a lot of vibration and rumbling, and with a loud roar off we go. It was dark and cold that night and it seemed like we were in the airplane a long time. Suddenly there was a thundering bang (humans call it a landing!) and the crates shuddered. I looked over at Charlie and Whitey and they looked back with a "should we be worried?" expression.

We eventually got unloaded and placed in a general holding area. Wow, this is nothing like the home I left in Kansas, the farm where I could run and play, the beautiful meadows, my siblings, my chickens, goats, and cow friends. They were nowhere to be seen. Right now, just me, the other dogs and lots of humans scrambling around.

Don't these people know we need to pee? We are dogs, that's what we do, especially in a new area and we don't know what to expect next. It's simple, we sniff, sniff, and pee, mark our new area and establish the pack pecking order. It's our primal instinct, to survive. Interestingly, so it is for humans.

That night while I was en route to Connecticut, Joe had no idea any of this was happening. What transpired was that his son Joey and daughter Jenna had "decided" (they thought they were in charge), it was time for mom and dad to have a puppy. What he didn't realize about this surprise was that Jenna or Joey weren't really doing this. It was, as he would learn, his Desire, magnetic attraction, and need for a spiritual guide in his life.

Little did he know at the time the value I, Kona, would serve and what was coming in his life. He had a family, friends, and a good job, so why did he still feel as though something was missing? I knew I had work to do here. I also knew he had limitations, self-imposed and hang-ups, as we all do. So, like it or not, the law of attraction moved all the forces, people, places, and things to help answer his focus and Desire.

Additionally, he did not know at the time that I, also needed him in my life. The reality is, we were both on a mission for each other and for God and others. Jenna, a remarkable musician, was a key instrument in helping that happen. You see, the discussion about spirituality, what alignment exists or doesn't between varying specie forms and why, was to be discovered.

So here comes this female human and her companion. She was by those standards, an attractive younger woman. She seemed to be totally excited to see me, picked me up, and started with what humans often do with puppies, squealing "You're so cute," and squeezing me. Don't they know we don't like the squeezing thing? It makes us feel trapped. In any event, I succumbed and gave her what she wanted; I licked her face, gave her rubs with my nose.

We moved outside into the cold and snowy night. The air stung, and even though I have longer fur, with a handsome light brown coat I might add, the wind had a real bite. We ended up in a car and all I *could see were the amazing differences from the house I just left in Kansas. We were in New York City, and through the frigid night air I could see millions of lights glistening against the snow. There were many very tall buildings and what is called concrete everywhere. No sign of grass, meadows, or farms. Fear struck me then, as I had no idea where we were going. Interestingly when Joe was a young boy, he wondered about direction and also found himself afraid.*

His mom Angela, while schooled in Roman Catholicism, always told him the important thing was to never leave Jesus. She didn't explicitly say it was okay to leave the church, but she was clearly emphasizing that following Christ trumped adherence to church doctrine. Her messaging, especially at challenging times of doubt, was consistent in reinforcing the point. She had an uncanny ability to understand all of us are connected in a deeper spiritual way, regardless of the configuration we are in here on earth.

Although in human form, she was as simple and humble a woman as Christ in many ways. She was loved by so many. She never held real contempt for others. She was always a cheerful person, always giving of herself.

Angela never abandoned Joe's father, for sixteen-plus years when he was disabled, and sacrificed so much for her three children. To know his mother was to know someone truly connected to Spirit and a remarkable Being.

When she was a little seven-year-old girl, back in the old country of Italy, in a small house in the southern town of Chiusano San Domenico, she became very ill with typhoid fever. In those days many humans died from that disease and the concerns about his mom surviving were real.

Angelina as she was referred to as a child, was ill for a long time. Her fever climbed to dangerous levels and the doctors couldn't get it down. Humans and dogs share many traits, including a narrow range for healthy body temperature. When it elevates beyond a certain level, known as "fever" or when it drops below normal, it is precarious. That night when I left Kansas, I became very cold, my paws were numb and my legs shivered.

Ultimately Joe's grandmother, friends, priests, and the community prayed for her. She was asleep one night and stopped breathing for a long period of time. The worries of all were realized and they acknowledged she had passed. She was alone in that bed while her mother was hysterical and others were doing their best to console her.

During this time, unbeknownst to the gathering, his mom vividly recalled seeing a bright white light and space, and then seeing a figure approaching her. She was convinced it was Mary, Jesus' mother. She approached mom with a loving smile and told her she had to go back, she had work to do, it wasn't time for her to come home.

The girl who would become Joe's mother began breathing and crying aloud and the congregation of people at the house were in amazement of what was certainly a miracle. In their minds (and in his mom's), the little girl had returned from death.

Well before my earthly experience, I watched his mother tell him that story in a quiet and unassuming way. This was an accounting she shared with very few people. I leave you to believe and interpret as you will. This isn't about convincing you to believe in miracles, to believe in the wonder and power of God, the Universe, Jesus.

Rather, to understand the undeniable processional effect of experiences and events, the meaning humans assign to them, and how they impact their lives and those around them. Angela lived her life with a level of commitment, discipline, selflessness, and responsibility that most who knew her would consider beyond human, truly of God.

As a young boy, Joe would often sit with her, sometimes late at night, and she would share many experiences and stories about her time in Italy and the convent. It never felt like a lecture about religion, rather a series of messages he would realize were powerful and mission-oriented. Angela just knew he needed to hear them at an early age. Heck I, and we all knew that!

She had to know what he would endure and achieve. She was strong, highly self-disciplined, tough, energetic, yet witty and funny. School, church, and honoring God were three of the most important things. She was relentless in ensuring nothing would be allowed to distract him or his siblings from them.

What then would he become? What then would he do to make her proud? What then did God expect of him and how would he manifest it? How will I play in this? Will I be relevant? Was he as selfish as he felt at the time? Are you? It is about self-actualization over time. It is not about perfection. It is about maintaining momentum to keep going.

Angela enjoyed great health most of her life and suffered a challenging last few years in a nursing home with dementia. I remember being taken there in those final months, snuggling up close to her as she petted me, feeling her remarkable love and spirit. I could tell through all my senses, Angela felt mine.

She would smile and I would smile back at her, her green hazel eyes connecting with my bulbous brown ones. Time seemed to freeze for her in those moments. For me, I was already, and am always, experiencing the moment.

Compared to his father, it was a merciful and relatively short period before her passing. When she was in the hospital and his brother John was sitting with her one evening, he beautifully captured the essence of who she was here on earth. Those lessons she taught Joe, his siblings, and others were:

All it takes to be happy is a home, some clothes, good food, and dignity.

The way to a successful life is simple. Be honest, be loyal, do the right thing, and know that you don't need much.

Every human interaction is joyous.

Every human being is valuable … the porter, the bus driver, the cashier.

Absolutely everyone responds to kindness. You will never be forgotten.

Absolutely nothing can defeat Faith in God.

No question the world is a better place for angelic Angela having been in it.

CHAPTER 2

Purpose

(KONA)

Joe's human father was very a creative artist. He painted and sculpted with passion. Later in his life Joe found that people were his creativity. He would bring his art form through coaching, mentoring, building businesses, relationships, heavy negotiations, and making deals. That sounds very practical and materialistic. Behind it is an insatiable driving force, a yearning to be aligned with a purpose, It was amazing to see how that works. But behind all this positivity and accomplishment, were obstacles, the limiting beliefs all humans face.

Many times they are buried deep within them, blocking their true potential, the powerful spiritual Force God gave them, and all spirits, regardless of form, that if channeled properly can move mountains. How do they find it? How does he and all humans deal with and get out of the ego mode that, while trying to protect, is at the same time judging, correcting and telling them what is not possible?

Often he felt the compelling desire to be, and enjoyed being, Mr. Popular. I get it, sort of like us canines in the pack. I see the world, with my large eyes from twelve inches above the ground in a silouhette of colors different than those of our human companions. Where we end up in the pack hierarchy is more than about size.

Why, then, was it so difficult at the time for him to look into the mirror? It was easy for him to look in the mirror at his head and hair, but not the rest of him. As an Italian-American teenager in the Bronx, and likely elsewhere, being "cool" and looking good mattered. That represented a part of, but not all of him.

Where might this show up in your life? The feeling of not being good enough; by whose standards do we ask that question? When does it really show up? I know there is a purpose for us all and sometimes it is not as complex as you think. It can be simple.

The journey is about remaining open and curious. Why do we dogs crave walks? It allows us to be inquisitive and in a state of wonderment. What new smells would we have today, how have our surroundings and conditions changed?

It requires a commitment to continuously improve all the time, to grow to love yourself, then others, in that order. It is not about the perfect "you" or "me." Just keep moving and going all the time at some pace.

The law of momentum; sometimes it is just one paw in front of the other, one foot in front of the other. If that is all you can muster, then so be it. We all share the 24/7 model, no more, no less. Why then do some human beings feel fully fulfilled and others are wobbly and bobbing around trying to find themselves? It is a process for all of them.

In those early days, before I was here in physical form, I remember a day when Joe was in Father Coyne's high school psychology class, where he felt drawn to understand human behavior. How did this all work? Was there more going on than appeared at the surface?

While his parents didn't provide specific career guidance, they wanted him to have a solid foundation. His scholastic abilities and their sacrifice enabled him to attend one of the best high schools, a Catholic school called Cardinal Spellman, in New York.

It was there that his exposure to interesting subjects and collection of friends started to dramatically improve. These were kids who, for the most part, had similar upbringing, and came from loving homes that required parental financial sacrifice to send them to the school.

So, this smart kid, who convinced himself he couldn't make a great living at psychology, leveraged his math and science prowess into a highly successful aerospace career. He grew up watching airplanes out of apartment windows, being fascinated with those flying contraptions.

He kept progressing but all throughout, even though gaining greater roles and increased responsibility, he felt something was still missing. Hmmm, did I feel something was missing too? Was Mr Popular lonely? Was I?

He felt partly empty inside. A cry out and belief that there was more to do? What was it? He had no governor at the time, no dad to help him gauge his life progress as a man, a father, and husband.

He was nearly 30 years old and felt that he hadn't accomplished much. He had a wife and two kids, a house, a career that enabled them to travel around the country working on the most advanced super-secret programs in the world! His closest pack friend Jimmy, aka "Cip," had asked him if maybe it was going too fast and should he slow down. His response was, think not, why stop, why wait?

He was aware, and I watched Joe's father work his whole life, marry late to Angela, have three kids, then end up with a long stay in a nursing home until he died. Why would Joe wait and do all this planning for tomorrow that might never arrive? Let's do it NOW!

Why not experience life to the fullest and not live with regrets wondering what if? Do you ever feel that way? Do you sometimes feel your life, and your efforts have been for everyone else and then what happens? Does life end? Watch fear creep up as you go?

Does the fear of not having enough morph into regrets for not doing or trying, and ending up in a bad place? Do you allow the outside world to drive you to what you should do, think, be? Where is the Trust?

There were so many signs in those days that he too worried about things that truly didn't matter. That was a time when he wouldn't allow dog hair on his couch! He didn't want pets in the house. It really wasn't about the hair. It is about focusing on importance and what really makes a difference. Although I might be seen by most as just a dog (a cute one for sure), I certainly would help change that viewpoint.

It is the energy that comes through them when they liberate themselves from the boundary conditions that were laid out for them. By whose standard? Ours? Others? Not the Divine One's, I suggest. The Universe notices intent. The "Universe" is God, Jesus, Mohammad, Buddha, whomever whatever you believe is the Universal Truth, the Being, the collective energy between us all.

A wonderful benefit of humans like Joe attending an engineering school is the study of energy, physics, and the quantum realm. Energy cannot be destroyed.

It can be changed and transformed into different phases, but not destroyed.

Your bodies, our bodies, are energy systems and magnetic. You attract experiences -- good or bad in your lives -- through focus and attention. This universal law is always in play whether you are aware of it or not. Do not be confused about the physical form you are in now. That's correct, dog, human, or other. This is a truth and if you study your life experiences you will see this was all about intent and what you were focused on.

CHAPTER 3

Trilogy

(JOE)

That cold December Christmas morning in 2008 was one I will always remember. We were opening gifts as always and I heard some commotion at the other end of the house. I could hear what I thought was a high-pitched bark. What was going on? Sure, it was Christmas, and running down the hall toward me was this little light-brown puppy! A dog in my house — are you kidding me! In the moment, I couldn't help but pick him up.

Wow, he was cute; black around his nose against a brown coat and light colored under-belly. He also had what some would say made him less than perfect, a cute and slightly crooked underbite. Of course he was less than perfect, a lesson right from the beginning! What kind of dog was he? It was obvious Jenna thought it was her plan to surprise us with our own dog. Little did she know, and certainly I didn't understand it at the time, but it was my manifestation.

He is what I desired and needed. How many times have situations existed where emotions, expressions showed up in your life and you had no idea why? You wondered how and where did this come from?

I thought the same about Kona. How could this be? I don't want a dog, I didn't want a dog. It is about focus with energy and emotion. When we say we "don't" with passion, we are at the same time sending the universe signals with our focus. The more we say "don't," by definition we are giving it focus and power, magnetically attracting it in our lives. It is why so often the things we tend to consciously resist end up showing up in our lives and may be precisely what we need at that moment.

Clearly for me, Kona was and would become a critical part of my journey. He would prove to be instrumental in closing the gap in what was missing in my life. He would grow and prove to be one of my life's greatest teachers and mentors!

He would allow me to be me, and to see myself for all I am and deserve to be. He would prove to be so much more than a "dog." He would help me love and laugh without restriction, without conditions, enable me to climb the highest mountains, to scream with fire and passion at all that mattered the most to me. To stop worrying about the crap that fills our minds and souls with emptiness, darkness, worry, fear.

He would be there for and with me through some of the most difficult times yet to come in my life, along with some of the most incredibly exhilarating moments. How could I have known?

When you face the fears of life and allow yourself to be open and less predictable, putting aside your own inhibitions, boundaries, limiting self-doubt and learn to trust, really trust, then you get in touch with the authentic you and will learn to know you and love you at a much bigger level.

It can be about the simple things in life, you know. Look at my mom who achieved her family, never had a checkbook or credit card, paid cash for everything, and lived in a modest apartment in the Bronx.

We eventually moved from the south Bronx when I was eleven, to a new apartment complex in the northeast section of the Bronx. We graduated from all five of us in a one-bedroom place to a sprawling two-bedroom apartment in a safer area of the city. Now Johnny and I had a bedroom to share. My sister slept on the pull-out sofa bed. This was the drill until my father became ill and was no longer home with us.

It was another typically cold January day and it was my freshman year of high school. Mid-term exams made it as stressful as all can imagine. My father had been encouraged to retire early from his time with the NYC Transit authority. He had logged more than thirty-eight years and with the Union benefits and pension plan, I guess he was better off if he retired. He was sixty-two years of age, with three kids under the age of thirteen. I certainly didn't understand all that at the time, and today's modern world of business has fewer of those financial options.

I do remember his behavior changing soon after he retired. He wasn't as patient and seemed lost, quiet, and depressed at times. I was busy being an inner-city teen and frankly was more concerned about me and my life. My mother had convinced him to see a doctor for an assessment. In our family, and maybe typical of those days, those situations were not shared with the kids, at least not in our traditional Italian-American house.

After some basic checks, my dad was admitted to a hospital for "observation" and rest, whatever that meant. He was there for about a week and I do remember talking to him on the phone; he was anxious to come home.

I returned home that life-changing afternoon from my last exam, to my find my mother hysterical and on the phone. She tried to explain something had happened to pop while he was at the hospital. It was all so confusing. He apparently had fallen down some stairs and hurt his spine.

Then the story changed to him having a heart attack. That seemed strange as I had been with him at the doctor not too long before and recall the doctor saying he had an amazingly strong heart; that of a much younger man. While he was a smoker, he also was heavily involved in exercise, worked out at the YMCA, and played tennis regularly.

Given the era, his regimen was more like that of that of a semi-pro or even a professional athlete. The story continued to unwind as he was being transported from a small hospital in Westchester County to the more comprehensive and highly rated New York hospital in Manhattan. By the time we arrived, we learned he was in a coma and apparently had the equivalent of a stroke. He had brain damage, the extent of which was still under evaluation.

As anyone who has had a similar situation of a parent or loved one knows, it was to say the least a dark day riddled with uncertainty. What did this all mean, how did it happen? He was fine the night before.

In the end, he spent several weeks in a coma and recovered with his left side fully paralyzed. He could not speak well and had a tracheotomy to breathe. My uncles and mother tried to understand what really happened and to this day, we have never learned the actual circumstances. The reality was, he would spend time in a rehab hospital and then the next sixteen years in a nursing home.

My mother, one of the toughest people I know, would be left to raise three young children alone in the city. She spent time with my father virtually every day for those sixteen years, save for the days you could count on two hands. Our Sundays had become church and visits with my father.

None of us has to look hard to find others with challenges equal to or greater than our own. What really matters is not the event or events, but the meaning we assign to them. Yes, I was angry, confused, frustrated, and rebellious. Later I grew to be grateful for the lessons I learned from my mother and her incredible honor, sacrifice, and love for her husband, God, and her family.

• • • •

(KONA)
The first few weeks were an adjustment period for all of us. I was busy sniffing and using my puppy paws and nails to scratch where I could. I got to meet my

new cousins. Tiki, he is a BUG, a Boston terrier/Pug mix. Now, I had to fit into a family with a BUG in it. He was brindle-colored with large puggy eyes and was a bit older than I.

He had boundless energy and since he was about the same size and weight, we would play all day until we were exhausted. Interestingly, Tiki was an important guide for Jenna and all she would later endure. For now, we were learning about each other and my home-sickness was fading away. I was learning the routine of my new pack family. Joe, the pack leader, was starting to seem comfortable with me and we did the typical "play with the puppy" thing.

He was a busy man and traveled on those metallic noise monsters called airplanes often. One of the very first lessons he would learn from me was about presence, and my letting him know how happy I was when he came home. I don't mean to occasionally show that, I mean always.

You see, one thing about these humans is the world around them often distracts them from being who they really are. It is not about the experiences; it seems more like they lose themselves and drift from what matters most. We dogs are far simpler than that. We know we want and need to have connection and are in the moment all the time.

As time went on in those early days, I would often get taken to a place called a puppy day-care. These human spirits have evolved to humanize canines to a great degree, but in the process sometimes forget we are spirits having a dog's life. This puppy day-care was a place where other dogs would be left for care and play while our pack leaders went on to work or social functions.

My relationship with Joe, the pack leader extraordinaire, was progressing well and I was wondering when he would realize what our relationship was all about. A first sign of his realization came early one morning. What he needed in his life now was to fully liberate himself from the trappings around him, the ability to let himself be fully himself around others, but mostly for himself. What he couldn't know was how important this would become later in his life.

At this point I didn't fully understand what I needed and why or what his mission was for me. I know I needed love and connection, though. And there was a third part of my mission and purpose that would take time for all to see. I was also serving as a communicator between our Creator and Joe, a conduit of sorts, and God too, had needs.

One of the things I learned early about him was that he was fascinated with his car and I would never go anywhere in it. It was a special fancy machine in which he took great pride. It was always remarkably clean and all I knew was Tiki and I would never get near or in it. I guess it really mattered to him.

In fairness, we do have paws with sharp nails and hair (mine much longer than Tiki's), and I guess that really matters? Or does it? How will that help him deal with the priorities and demands he will soon need to make in his life? Or was his car a distraction? He wasn't able to necessarily see it, and my job was to help him break it down.

As I grew to know him, I could see he was clearly a great pack leader, always watching out for his human family and other creatures as well. Here is an example of how resistance in humans doesn't signify who they really are. Their focus can be misaligned.

There was this other creature in our house, a small white animal called a ferret. His name was Weebs. Weebs spent most of his time in a crate of sorts. Joe didn't really appreciate the albino-looking critter. I get that, and feel privileged, as I felt he wasn't sure he liked me early on.

Little did I know how much he would grow to love me and to ultimately realize that our meeting was not one of chance, no not at all, rather by design, attraction, and need, leading to eventual manifestation, critical to our future to enable us to carry out our mission. We would experience how different species can in fact be spiritual beings, first living out a mortal experience in varying forms.

One night, Weebs somehow managed to get out of his crate and the entire pack was looking frantically for him. They looked everywhere in the house and couldn't find him. They became convinced he had escaped the house; it was brutally cold and the grounds were covered with frozen snow. It was night and it would be nearly impossible to see his white coat against the crystallized snow.

As time went on and the pack feared the worst, Joe was staring out the window and then happened to see Weebs running across the lawn! Joe immediately ran outside without a coat and looked around every corner, bush, and crevice and eventually found Weebs desperately trying to re-enter the house. Joe picked him up and carried the small, cold animal into the house. Here was a simple example of the real man: empathetic and caring, but sometimes masked by other things we think matter.

Living in the moment is not some mystical view of being blind to everything around you. Don't you all want to climb to the top of the mountain to see the view? To scream out with exhilaration at the abundance you see and get to experience? What is that mountain or lake-view for you?

You deserve so much but need to get out of your own way to allow the God force to come through and believe in why you were created. If you are not sure of what you ultimately want, then be grateful for all you have, including the trials and tribulations, pain, challenges, and judgments.

Certainly we should appreciate the feelings of joy, happiness, family and friends, and love for all of the creatures here with us. Yes, all the creatures, spirit ones, were sent here as well.

It is through periods of suffering you will get closer to your soul and learn there is even a deeper level.

CHAPTER 4

—

Kona

My name is Kona, yes that's Kona with a K, like the beautiful place in Hawaii and the great coffee. I am, by dog standards and definition, a small, muscular combination of what is known as a Jack Russell and Pug mix. They call me a "Jug." Yes, that's right. I am 50% Jack so that dominates much of my personality.

This is my story now, too. It is about the level of spiritual connectivity between two very different physical species with Desired intent. The story and relationship between a spirit in human form and a special spirit in dog form and what and why are both here in this space and time. It is about purpose, mission, teachings, laughter, love, light ... so say hi to me, Kona!

Joe would evolve and ultimately tell people that I am one very special creature. He would eventually realize with no doubt in his mind that he manifested me, Kona, to come into his life at a time and place that was supposed to happen, that had to happen.

Yes, by many people's view, I am a a dog – but not just any dog but a special guide. This is a story about how the Universe can deliver spiritual guidance all humans need. We are all here to learn, to grow, to experience, to ultimately go for it and live a life of passion and power to reach our highest and best.

So, this pack leader of mine, Joe, has a real thing for hiking and playing in the mountains. He especially likes to go in the winter time. Part of the reason he called for me and I was sent to him in my current form is the Jack Russell part of me is very agile, high-energy with good solid endurance.

I don't have the full smushed Pug face, so I can breathe easier when I run. I can show him the way through the rocks and boulders (where else in his life will I do this?). When he slows to ponder the way to go, I'm often the one in front and instinctively and intuitively finding the path forward.

There certainly are other breeds of dogs that are comfortable doing this outdoor stuff, but I have been packaged to be a complete guide, emotionally, spiritually, and physically. The Pug part of me is perfect for him too! He really has two speeds, fast and stop. So do I. The Pug keeps me from allowing my "Jack" side to overpower and perhaps not take the time to show patience and to relax. How can I teach him to relax and enjoy the moment if I, too, am always on the go? That wouldn't be spiritual connection.

I am all about the mission. Oh yes, but I have needs too! Will he realize why we both are on missions? For each other and for God? It is a spiritual Trifecta ... three of us, Spirit in different forms, locked in together, all with jobs to do and with needs to be met.

CHAPTER 5

Firewalk

(JOE)

Back in 1998 I remember my first experience at a Tony Robbins event, a multi-day seminar called "Unleash the Power Within" (UPW). Wow, I thought, was this going to be a stretch! I signed up for this seminar while watching a late-night TV infomercial. I bought an audio tape set first, and as I listened I became curious and intrigued.

There was all this promise about "unleashing the power within you" and something about doing a fire walk! Well now, the physics, math, and engineer in me suggested there would have to be some physical protection and/or a trick. Humans don't/can't walk on one thousand-degree plus hot coals!

In any event I was certainly searching for higher levels of performance in my personal and professional life, and like all of us, I had some behaviors I wasn't proud of. I was overall in a "good" space when I attended the event, though. I went alone, and have to say, upon arrival I was confused and frankly thinking, what the hell am I doing here!? Feels like a cult, etc.

There was loud music (I love music, it gets me into a flow, makes me feel happy and free) lots of people "high fiving" each other and jumping around, smiling and clapping. There were many people like me, first timers and also what at first blush looked like "groupies." I committed to the four-day event and it began.

After a lot of Tony talks providing the foundation on understanding our emotions and how they really work, he explained how we really "do" emotions to ultimately either avoid pain or gain pleasure. He helped us understand how our choosing to "do" emotions versus them just happening to us was based on a number of factors. We then went on to prepare for the fire walk.

In the end we did in fact walk barefoot across those hot burning coals! It is possible with some basic training and focus. Here we go again: what you focus on is what you get.

We were coached to use a mantra that would allow our conscious minds to focus on something "cool" versus "hot." Repeating the mantra, it kept the ego from saying, "Hey stupid, you're going to get burned!" The experience was exhilarating and somewhat exhausting.

It wasn't so much the physical aspect of walking on fire, it was the dealing with the obstacle, the fear, the uncertainty, the anxiety on the one side of making things bigger than they are, and the fantastic feeling on the other side after crossing the bed of coals.

The firewalk was and is a metaphor for life! It is about bridging from the things that hold us back, the monsters we create, and to then realize that what seemed to be perhaps physically impossible to the logical mind was and is totally possible and may be much easier than we first thought.

You can go walk on fire if you want. Do something to break down past and current limiting beliefs. Do something that is well outside your comfort zone. Build those emotional muscles and continue to develop conditioned responses into your nervous system, from which you will automatically draw power.

How about using it to anchor self-love, self-appreciation into yourself? To be able to go to a place where you can call on these resources to serve you at any time in any given situation.

There are plenty of ways to learn more about anchoring. It is used every day in marketing and advertising and affects us all. It is about wiring an emotional state into our nervous system. An easy way to remember it is, "At the peak, do something unique." When we are in a heightened emotional state -- like nine or ten on a scale of ten -- and a unique touch or sound is made, the state is wired to our nervous system.

That touch and or sound become a trigger to set off that particular emotion in the future. It varies with the degree of intensity and the repetition. Have you ever noticed a major shift in how you feel when you hear a certain song or experience a particular smell?

You wonder what just happened; likely some anchor was triggered. You can use anchoring to help change your state.

The first event was only the beginning. I felt like a changed man, expanded in many ways, enlightened and exhilarated, but wondered if the feelings would last when life showed up? In some ways I pondered if it would be like a great party or concert where you escape from reality temporarily and have a great time. What then? What would people think? Was Joe, aka Mountain Man, now in some "feel good" cult? He was always a positive guy but what the heck happened to him?

One great example of an early change was my attitude and behavior with a cat we had, named Cleo. We just never really got along so well, but after the UPW event all seemed to change. I started to not only have a greater tolerance for her but also really appreciate her. She in turn reciprocated and we enjoyed each other until she passed at age seventeen. I broke down weeping.

I immediately began engaging in several Tony Robbins events. I volunteered to be a crew member at multiple UPWs, signed up for Mastery University and then Trainer Academy all within a year of my first event. Mastery University was an amazing journey of personal development. Mastery U consisted of three parts: Life Mastery, Wealth Mastery, and Date with Destiny, each of which ranged in length from four to ten days. The program was typically completed within a one- to two-year period.

Life Mastery, focused on the mind and physical body, internal and external, including nutrition, exercise, meditation and experiences to push you well beyond your comfort zone. Wealth Mastery was all about a variety of strategies, and investment approaches to build, retain, and protect wealth. Date with Destiny was designed as a deep introspective self-discovery process to learn who we really are, and find our true Desire and Purpose.

All were pieces of the puzzle and the process that I couldn't see at the time. It was all coming together, but slowly. The journey and the mission were well under way.

During Life Mastery, there were many exercises and physical challenges to help you grow, and improve the physical aspects of your body and mind. This included up-to-date nutritional guidance and exercise.

CHAPTER 6

Bliss

(KONA)

After completing Mastery University, Joe went on to work as a volunteer coach, crew, and trainer at several events. Date with Destiny was one of the most outstanding experiences for him and he loved going back to support others in their journey.

There is one specific story I'll share that had a profound impact on him. It is an amazing example of how a person could be happy, truly blissful, despite what he and most others would consider incredible limitations.

The entire event was designed to be introspective and a dive in getting to know oneself at the deepest level. There is where humans find their truest Desire, their fears, their inner voice singing, laughing, or crying, telling them they can, or cannot. It is a process requiring vulnerability, openness, and trust.

At this event there was a gentleman in a wheelchair, a full quadriplegic literally sipping water through a straw. Although we canines need all four limbs to walk, or we dogs and humans think we do. This man could not walk or touch or feel anything.

We dogs have an acute sense of smell that helps us navigate in many ways. We can sense energy in humans and other beings instantly. The empathetic humans in the venue were saddened by his apparent physical limitations.

He was eventually invited to share his story. The specifics aren't so important, but what is compelling is how he described his true bliss. He was truly happy, and it was all based on love. He loved himself for all he had and was grateful for everything in his life. He said all the experiences in his life, yes including the loss of his motor functions, were an important part of his evolution as he moved to higher levels of consciousness and with less distractions, moved closer to his Creator.

While his experiences and sharing were inspirational and intellectually helpful to attempt to appreciate his bliss, what amazed Joe and impacted him the most was the one or two seconds where time slowed down and virtually stopped for him. He could "understand" and feel exactly how the man in the wheelchair felt. He literally experienced the joy and happiness that man had. It was a remarkable, life-changing moment for him. Why?

It was a glimpse at what was possible when we move past our physical obstacles and get in touch with our Spirit, who we really are and how much God loves us. It is no longer about judgments and self-imposed feelings of inadequacy.

Contrast is also a powerful tool; In that microcosm of a moment when he understood how a quadriplegic man could be truly blissful, it made him realize that so much of what he was carrying --his father's plight, his mom and her load, his feeling deprived -- all seemed insignificant.

You are right where you are supposed to be even when it doesn't feel that way*. Just know and trust that is what is really going on. Accept love, cherish every moment in time, no matter the external circumstance.*

Much like light, you cannot move to where you want, or desire to be, from a place of resistance. A room doesn't go from dark to light without a switch! It can be a challenge to be grateful for your, and our every trial and tribulation, but only then can we unblock the true potential. It is key to be okay with where you are right now. It is as it must be.

Before my time here on earth, there were many learning experiences for Joe, the Mountain Man. While I wasn't yet in Kona form at the time of that Date with Destiny event, it helped him and me prepare for the mission. That suspended moment in time helped shape many of his views and how he interpreted events later in his life.

He often refers to life being analogous to an old-fashioned pinball machine. It is a game many human children, and adults, play. Canines also play games for fun and often there are deeper meanings for us, as for all spirit forms.

If you think about it, all humans in their own way want to hit the jackpot in the pinball game. Just check the excitement of a child watching the pinball make its way throught the maze, and the flashing lights, bells, and whistles. They want to hear that buzzer, they want the prize! Don't they? Sure they do!

Think about the bumpers on the table of the machine. When they launch the ball, as it tries to make its way up the table through the series of flippers, it bangs and gets knocked around, often bouncing off many bumpers. If that ball represents them in life, when you crash into a "bumper" and get redirected, sometimes in a counter-direction from the jackpot, and it hurts, realize your Divine Creator, your God, Universe, whatever Supremacy you believe in, has placed those bumpers there based on your own mag-netic attraction.

They aren't intended to hurt or block you, no, no, rather to help guide you to the jackpot! It is a naviga-tion map, filled with challenges and impacts from us, but with the intent for all of you to hear those buzz-ers ring, those lights to flash brightly, to know yes

yes dearest love, a wonderful extraordinary creation born out of God's need for love too, for His desire to not be alone, to marvel at this vast universe alone, to help steer you to the ultimate prize!

It is why when you look back at difficult events, after the fact, you often realize their real meaning and value.

CHAPTER 7

The Staircase

(JOE)

In the mid-to-late 1970s in New York City, street gangs were prevalent. Kids and teens were looking for ways to connect and find significance and worthiness, that powerful popularity to help them feel special. Yes, me too -- talk about a paradox. Here is an Italian-American kid, with a Catholic, strict mom who was raised in a convent in Italy, as tough as a drill sergeant, yet I found my way through rebellion and pain to connect with those who were not becoming of a son she could be proud of, even through so much love, connection and prayer.

There were many gangs based on ethnicity and some territoriality. I was part of a mostly all-Italian-heritage group in the Bronx. Organizational structure varied but we had our own version of divisions, like some quasi-paramilitary team. In the area of the Bronx we lived, there were rival gangs that clearly out-numbered us and our division was a smaller detachment compared to other areas of the Bronx.

One day my buddies and I were "hanging out" in a staircase. This was typical behavior for teens living in high-rise apartment buildings ranging from twenty-four to thirty-three flights. We were being mischievous and decided to run down the stairwell, knocking out light bulbs. It certainly wasn't good behavior but was harmless overall. I was the last kid in the group of about seven of us.

Suddenly, I felt someone grab me from behind and I at first assumed it was my buddy Stevie. I had lost track of where everyone was once we started the procession down. I was immediately turned around and slammed hard up against the inside of an exit door. I wasn't sure what floor we were on but was absolutely clear who my accosters were. It was a group of six guys from a notoriously tough and feared rival gang with dominance in the area. This was not good!

They wanted to know who I was with, the names of my cohorts, where we met, what were our plans etc. I refused to give any info, which was rewarded with unmerciful blows to my face and head.

One of their leaders asked me about a gold chain and necklace I was wearing. It was the Madonna my mother had given me. They wanted me to surrender it, along with the names and info on our gang meetings. I continued to refuse and paid a terrible price.

They ripped the medal and chain off which resulted in a massive reaction from me. I had no chance with a six-to-one ratio. It was a terrible beating, blood everywhere.

The mercy in the event was my recollection of one guy who never hit me but repeatedly called to "let's throw the Motherfucker ... down the stairs" It was almost like a mantra. I thank God that never happened.

● ● ● ●

(KONA)

While in canine form, I certainly live the pack life. I understand the confusion Joe experienced. He wondered, where were his guys? Surely, they knew he was missing? Did they abandon him? Did God abandon him? Why and how was this happening to him? Here he was being loyal and no one came back to look for him?

He eventually crawled out of the building and upon seeing one of the local security guards, passed out. He ultimately recovered from what was bad bruising, cracked ribs, and a concussion but with no permanent physical damage. It was a lesson in loyalty. He never surrendered the information, nor did he or does he regret not doing so.

Interestingly many years later when his son Joey was a little boy, he would spend nights at Joe's mother's house. He loved his grandmother, his Nonna. His mother's apartment was in a building near the location where the dreadful beating occurred many years before.

One night, when little Joey was probably around five or six years old, he woke up in the middle of the night at Nonna's screaming about a nightmare he was having. He told Joe's mother, in excruciating detail (well beyond what one would expect from such a young boy), of seeing his dad getting beat up in the very building where it occurred! Joe never spoke about that story to many people and certainly not to his little boy. How could his son little Joey know?

We are all connected. Kona, Joe and his Spirit, his mission, my mission are real. Energy is always in play. It was such an extraordinarily emotional event.

There are lessons in every experience; often more so in the painful ones. He wondered was it worth it? Should he have just given them what they wanted, what's the big deal about names and meeting times anyway? Where were his pack "friends" now? We canines, the epitome of a pack get it. We too often wonder and feel abandoned.

While he was there in the staircase, alone being pummeled, fighting to stay conscious, all the while holding on to his values, his principles, curious was it worth it? He certainly didn't feel like a tough guy.

What may have seemed like a shallow expression of loyalty based on a teenager's attempt to be tough, was in actuality a strengthening of a deep core value. Loyalty has been a staple of his character ever since.

There have been so many times in his life since that brutal day that he refused to compromise his principles and values. It has served him well, even *when it drove him to make changes such as leave what was perceived to be great corporate jobs. His values and principles drive him, as all humans, to certain behaviors.*

The most powerful force in the human personality is the need to remain consistent with the identity we hold for ourselves.

● ● ● ●

(JOE)

I believe God intervened, and yes, helped me that day. While I was angry at Him for my family situation, at the same time I started to learn (from mom) that beyond the dogmatic nonsense of bureaucratic religion and church, the pure message of Ask and you will Receive was there! Yes, it is true.

We are all driven by four primary human needs supported by two foundational ones. The need for love/connection; significance; certainty; uncertainty/variety are the primary and are met no matter what. The way we meet them can vary greatly. The other two are growth and the need to contribute.

Today it is clear and easy to comprehend the attraction of a "gang." It meets the primary needs quickly and easily. The unfortunate downside is the class of those experiences. Think about how we would experience that at the highest level. To be significant in a way God would love and appreciate is; if it felt good, was good for you, was good for others and served the greater good.

As an example, some men, knowing that miraculous point in time, when the odds were statistically stacked way against them, when that specific sperm fought its way and survived to connect with that egg at that precise moment, a one in ten or fifteen million chance, is more than enough to know their uniqueness, their beauty, their divine connection, their purpose.

For others, when they kick the dog, beat the wife physically or emotionally, lash out, exude their power and authority, beat up other gang members, carry weapons to feel powerful. In both cases, the human need to be significant is met. Clearly, we know which one is empowering and desired. We can apply the same approach to meeting the other needs. Something to think about....

CHAPTER 8

—

Jackpot

(JOE)

At Trainer Academy, in 1998, I met an extraordinary man named Jim. We would be partners for the weekend. Jim was an established foot doctor and surgeon in northern California and we connected well and fast. We would go though many experiences together, designed to help us learn and get in touch with the coach within us.

First, we needed to flush out our own beliefs and limitations, and learn to share our vulnerabilities. We worked on and learned to diagnose a person's issue (what was really going on), how to help walk through a change process that includes coaching, empowering alternatives, conditioning, testing and creating a supportive environment for lasting change.

At the time we met, Jim was facing challenges related to commitment, specifically marriage, and I was dealing with wanting and needing to attain a closer and deeper relationship with my young son. We worked hard using the tools to help each other and developed a strong bond that continues to strengthen today.

Jim and I have been very close friends, more like brothers from different mothers, for more than twenty years. Amazingly though, the process after the Academy was such that we didn't see each other for many years. We built our deep relationship largely remotely in the first decade. We engaged through phone calls and eventually through the internet with emails, etc.

How was it possible to not only maintain, but truly grow a relationship, a brotherhood, 3,000 miles apart with no personal interaction between two men with vastly different backgrounds? We were, and are in fact, spiritually connected as many of us are in life.

Jim married beautiful Susan and has two wonderful and gorgeous girls today. My son and daughter are grown up and we often reminisce and think about the many experiences, how fast the time flew by and how we truly grew to love and appreciate each other and our families.

We have leaned on each other through the years especially through some difficult times we both have faced. He is a vital part of the story and my journey and I have no doubt, he is a God-send, a loving angel in my life, who is ever present for me, who I can reach out to and share my deepest thoughts, concerns, and feelings without judgment and with love.

I remember the first time I saw Jim after about a ten-year absence. He picked me up at the airport and we were sort of like kids who were pen pals. We both felt a little anxiety. While we certainly grew and built a relationship remotely, how would it feel to actually be together?

I came into the baggage-claim area and there he was waiting. It was awesome to see him and we quickly tooled off in his new Porsche 911. Wow, it felt like we had just been together at Trainer Academy.

It was a great first visit to their house when Priscilla and Marissa were little girls. I was proud and thankful he smashed past his inhibition around marriage commitment and was now blessed with such a beautiful family. I recall waking up that morning and standing at the top of the stairs looking down at sweet little Marissa. She stared up at this strange man in the house, who is that giant guy, and why is he here! We had a wonderful time.

CHAPTER 9

The Jetway

(JOE)

I remember when I graduated college and left New York for my first job in California. I was stricken with fear and uncertainty as how this would turn out. My beautiful strong mother showed no emotion prior to my leaving, even to the point where I wondered if she would miss me.

She had such inner strength and was battle-hardened from the grueling commitment to my father. I felt pangs of guilt about leaving. She was proud of me and told me I needed to go. Was I abandoning her? Was it all about me? What was the point of staying home? It was time for me to get moving with my life and no one wanted that more than my mom.

While it was many years ago now, leaving on the airplane that day was a pivotal moment in my life. It was about letting go, taking action, fighting against emotions and fear, and starting to visualize a future that was bright and fulfilling. Away from the painful memories, the behaviors, the feeling of confinement, the feeling of Desire was born within me to do more than average and to defy the odds.

I vividly remember my brother and sister telling me that while I was still likely walking down the jetway bridge, my mother broke down, hysterically crying and nearly collapsed. Here she was watching her firstborn go off to start a life, a better life, away from the trappings of the city and finally allowing herself to step back from her power and strength and feel the emotion of separation.

The lack of ambition around me, those people who weren't good for me, didn't really make me feel good, and didn't serve that greater good, but helped me find the inner strength and courage to take a bold step and move to California at age twenty.

Nonetheless, leaving my mom with my siblings, and the guilt of my father in a nursing home were buried deep inside me, although I didn't see it at the time. It was there for sure. Interestingly, Kona was experiencing a similar situation so many years later, on that winter night in Kansas.

• • • •

(KONA)

I know most people would say I am just a dog and it is not the same. Let's do a faith check here; who is to know then what experience is real? Spirits having human or non-human experiences? Spirit having a "dog" experience? Could it be there is more alignment, more connection? Should we always discount what we don't know for sure? Where else does this show up in our lives?

Amazingly humans seem to think they are just that, humans. Some of us believe for sure that we also enjoy some spirituality and the associated experience. Some of us might actually believe we are spiritual beings having a physical experience.

Is it then that God or whatever you believe created you, sent us here and allowed you to be in human form? Is it then that is the only form to enjoy, explore, experience spirituality? What about other forms -- the fish, the fowl, the many species of non-human animals? What are they? Are they simply the same then, non-humans having or not having a spiritual experience? Or is it even possible they are spirits having a "dog" experience? Yes, the good looking dog named Kona!

What, and how does the law of attraction work here? Who knows what we need most in our life? Is it us? How then or what then would we attract in our lives if in fact we desire to be loved, to be wanted, to be worthy, to be needed, to matter to God, to matter to those we love? What would we manifest into our existence?

What would help us to not focus on the pain or pleasure of the past so much or to focus on the potential future? How do we enjoy the beauty of the moment? How is it possible, or is it possible, to live and be present fully in the moment? Can it be learned? What is time after all? Who measures it? Why do so many humans feel like they don't have enough of it?

*Let me suggest that in the end, **time is really a feeling.** It helps explain why doing different events or tasks or situations can make time seem to stand still or "fly by." Yes, we dogs live in the moment as a general rule.*

So many programs and processes are designed to help teach and coach humans to find ways to be more present in the moment. Countless self-help books, seminars, and coaches have been created to work this phenomenon. These all can be powerful tools and helpful. If for no other reason, these help validate the deep desire we have to connect with the moment, to slow/stop, if possible, when experiences are positive and to wish it away when we are challenged.

CHAPTER 10

We're not in Kansas Anymore

(KONA)

After a long drive, we end up pulling into a driveway of a house. Wow, this place didn't look at all like Kansas. Here we go again, she grabs me, snuggles me by squeezing me, wraps me in a blanket, walks up the path and we enter the house. I had the full wiggle going until she realized it was "potty" time. We need to pee and poop. She took me back outside, put me down in the cold snow and let me relieve myself. Oh, that felt soooo good!

I would love to have started to check out the property, but it was cold and apparently there was a plan. This was just the beginning of the longer story. Tonight was about the little "secret."

I was brought into the warm house, I could smell a wood-burning stove, they had a large one and it reminded me a little of home. I met the other sibling, Joey, a big version of this homo-sapiens class, large muscles and strong.

He did the same squeeze thing on me but I reacted a little differently. Puppies like me have razor sharp puppy teeth and as I lunged a bit to lick his face I scraped his rather large Romanesque nose.

It became evident that my showing up was unknown (at least consciously) to my eventual spiritual partner. He at the time wanted nothing to do with dogs, too much "hair," hassle, time, etc. They snuggled me away in one of the bedrooms and kept doing the "shhhh be quiet thing."

The morning came fast, and it was a holiday, Christmas, when many humans celebrate the birth of the Enlightened One, Jesus Christ. It was a big thing back in Kansas, so I understand.

There was a large tree, why was it in the middle of the house? I had no idea but what I was sure of is I needed to get a sniff of it and give it a pee! It was important, if this was to be my new home then I needed to mark it so there was no confusion. Yep, this is now Kona's place!

• • • •

The Summer Solstice

It was an amazing day back in 2008, a critically important day in Mountain Man's journey, months before I was created in the form of the "Southy" Irishman, the Jack of all Jacks, the spirit he so wanted and needed -- before I arrived in dog form. The mission was in play, the manifestation conceived and attracted by him and Him.

Joe has an insatiable desire to be in nature, in the mountains, climbing them to be specific, because well they are there, they represent a step toward achieving one's highest and best, to escape the doldrums of everyday human distraction, to attempt to spend time in the moment, to enjoy the abundance, have fun, and be adventurous. Most humans have a funny way of relaxing!

So my design was no coincidence. I am low to the ground, muscular I might add, although some of these homo sapiens refer to me as thick in the middle. I was put together with keen agility and excellent navigation skills. My instincts were sharp and proactive and the innate ability for a Jack to sometimes worry, would serve as an alarm bell, that is if he would stop to pay attention!

In June of that year, he and his wonderful human wife partner Mo, I call her Mom D, decided to go to one of their favorite places, the White Mountains of New Hampshire. They were in the process of climbing what was referred to as the forty-eight four-thousand footers.

The "Whites" are rugged, rocky and steep, and they had set out to do a traverse of the Presidential ("Presi") range. The plan was to enjoy the summer solstice on top of the highest peak in the Northeast, Mt. Washington.

It was summer and while he knew the range well, as he had spent years climbing in that area, he and his partner, his wife, were not prepared for that day and night! It had to happen though, for me, the trail ambassador extraordinaire, to be called to duty.

• • • •

(JOE)

Our plan was to start at the Pinkham lodge parking area and climb Mt. Madison, spend the night at the high-mountain hut and then proceed over Adams, Jefferson, and onto Washington the next day.

It being early summer, the threat of thunderstorms with heavy rain and wind or blinding snow and hail was possible. The Presi range, and Mt. Washington specifically, is known for having the world's worst weather, at any time of the year.

It is the geography and convergence of multiple storm tracks that are the major responsibility for this behavior and reputation. Many have died due to exposure above tree line even in summer. The prevailing winds are typically from the west/north west (especially in winter) and the natural layout of the mountains create a Venturi effect.

The Venturi effect is the phenomenon that occurs when a fluid that is flowing through a pipe is forced through a narrow section, resulting in a pressure decrease and a velocity increase. The effect is mathematically described by principle and equation defined by a famous physicist known as Bernoulli, back in the 1700s. It can be observed in both nature and industry.

In the case of Mt. Washington, the topography, particularly on the west side, acts like a narrowing pipe where the wind picks up speed due to the natural formation.

The combined venturi effect with the higher elevation, forces the winds to pick up to extraordinary speed. It is "normal" for Washington to have sustained winds well over 80 mph and gusts well over 100 mph at any time of the year. In fact, the highest wind ever recorded in the world and verified by a human was on Mt. Washington, 231 mph back in 1934!

My wife, Mo and I had prepared our gear meticulously, given the respect we held for this region. I had been climbing here since my scouting days. The morning of departure was hotter and more humid than normal for a late June day.

We checked the latest forecast and while the threat of afternoon storms existed, with moderate winds gusting from 40 to 50 mph at the peaks, there were no warnings to avoid climbing above tree line.

After filling up with extra water due to the unseasonable heat and humidity, doing a final check, we started out northward targeting Mt. Madison. Our packs were heavier than usual due to the water load and multi-day excursion and our discipline to carry cold-weather gear despite the sultry start.

Mo seemed tired that morning and she typically struggles at the beginning, especially when it's hot. The trail set we chose would take us though some flat, heavily forested areas through part of the Great Gulf Wilderness, an area remarkably feeling untouched by humans despite its relative proximity to civilization. We would then begin an arduous and very steep climb over a set of false summits before finally summiting Madison.

We were perspiring heavily due to the high humidity and Mo seemed to be frustrated to find her cadence. The winds were picking up with some rain showers forcing us to make some adjustments to our gear. As we approached the tree line, I remember looking to the south and west and seeing Mt. Washington, its summit drifting in and out of the clouds.

That day it looked ominous and intimidating more than majestic. Amazingly now, years later, I know my internal guidance system was working, sounding a soft alarm, that I missed or chose to ignore. **It is in those micro moments that we get a sense, a feeling, an intuition, to which we must pay attention**.

We continued to climb with a few breaks over each of the false summits. There are arguably three on the trail we chose on the way to Madison. The terrain above tree line became rugged to say the least, with large rocks and boulders. We slogged our way upward with multiple clothing and gear changes due to the varied weather.

For the most part, we had good visibility for the White Mountains, with mostly overcast skies and light to medium winds gusting to 40+ mph. All in all, this is considered a good weather hiking day in New Hampshire! We were drinking more water than usual and balancing it with higher doses of electrolytes to ensure our biochemistry remained in a good place.

After about eight tough miles we made it to the Madison summit! It was really getting windy, with 50 to 60 mph gusts and a prevailing southwesterly flow. Not a good sign in the summer.

After celebrating, taking in some food and resting, we continued along the ridge to summit Mt. Adams. All the while I kept looking over toward Washington, with its broad and monstrous summit. We could see the top less now due to the lower ceiling.

We were excited to spend the summer solstice on top, but my inner feelings of uneasiness were growing. What was going on? I know these mountains and their unpredictability. Certainly, we were prepared and know the rules. The mountain will always be there, and we would execute our exit strategy if weather demanded it ... surely we would.

After a laborious day we were exhilarated, exhausted and happy to be at the Madison high-mountain hut for the night. Due to the fragile alpine growth (it takes years for the vegetation to grow even an inch) no camping is permitted above tree line except in designated locations or if there is a two-foot base of snow. We relished the idea of a crude bunk and a hot meal! After some light reading and journaling the highlights of the day, we were fast asleep.

When we woke in the morning around 6 a.m., we both felt a bit sore and achy from the strenuous trek the day before. The heat and humidity did a job on our electrolyte balance despite the supplementation.

It looked gloomy out and overcast with typical above-tree-line winds. The humidity was high and the wind, while swirling some, did seem to have a prevailing southwesterly flow. Hmmmm, that meant more moisture and it was in fact the summer solstice.

Our plan was to continue hiking the ridgeline trail south over the rest of the daunting and craggy Presidential peaks until we reached and summited Mt. Washington.

It was a Sunday morning, and most hikers at Madison had hiked the northern route and would be descending. There is no right or wrong direction to hike the traverse. Most first-timers tend to go north. We had done the northern trek some eight years earlier and thought it would be exciting to see the terrain from the opposite direction.

I walked outside the hut and found myself staring at the grey sky and sensing the moisture. The AMC (Appalachian Mountain Club), and local rangers do a great job in constantly reporting and updating weather forecasts due to the volatile nature of the region.

As we always do, we checked with the hut master and read the updated report for the high summits. It basically called for increasing winds later in the day, rain and thunderstorms possible mostly to the west. It did not contain any stern warnings for above the tree line. We assumed it was the latest and updated report. Later we would learn that was a flawed assumption.

• • • •

(KONA)
So here he was back then, so adept at the mountains and the outdoors, but in fact he wasn't paying full attention to his intuition, his internal guidance system. These humans, and this soon-to-be my human,

my project, my desire, my mission, was smart but needed a navigation beacon. He needed a "trail ambassador," he needed me!

At the time he and Mo were up there in those mountains, I was in Spirit form waiting and readying for what was next. It would be a short time now before I, Kona, would get my mission!

He could and would learn from a soon-to-be-badass- little southy canine who would instinctively know and sense danger. We are so much more in touch with energy and fields. We get the pack; who is where and why. I would help him find the way through the "boulders."

• • • •

(JOE)

After breakfast, we gathered our gear, packed up and set off on the southerly route. A route that would bring anxiety, worry, fear, and real danger! It always takes a mile or so the day after a tough climb to find your stride and feel loosened up. My body was feeling better, but I found myself edgy and impatient, really pushing the tempo.

Mo noticed it and was struggling to keep up and was bothered by my uncharacteristic behavior. I was, in fact, starting to worry. The trail was fully exposed to the weather with little opportunity for shelter. Additionally, there were a few miles with no real bail-out trails or means of escape below the tree line. There are steep drop-offs, some with very dangerous and perilous descents in even fair weather, not to mention in storms with high winds.

It is so easy to lose one's confidence and trust when fear arrives, the uncertainty of the moment, the feeling of responsibility to protect the loved ones, in this case my wife.

Yes, our behaviors can change in different ways to cope, to deal with the lack of trust, in ourselves, our God.

Although Kona was not in my physical life yet, he was in fact spiritually in play. The simple, handsome, loving, energetic dog was a protector. The inner wolf never left the domesticated dog regardless of the number of generations. They continue to be wired to protect their pack. God does too. It was and is His promise, sent in many ways and forms.

As we made our way from the hut toward a place called Thunderstorm Junction, the skies looked darker to the west and the winds, while certainly moderate for the range, were picking up. The junction is where three different storm tracks converge and are in part responsible for the hellacious weather that can form in minutes.

The temperature was still mild and humid but with the wind and some rain, I was worried about us getting wet and then chilled on the long and exposed trek. I was likely grating on Mo's nerves, as I demanded she put on her wind and rain protection. As is typical, we would end up making several stops to either add or remove clothing in an effort to regulate our body temperature and perspiration.

Having spent so much time in these mountains, knowing and respecting them and their potential for violent unpredictability, how was it that we were in this deteriorating situation? It is always about decision-making and pre-planning, what is the exit strategy and alternate routes for rapid descent, etc.

I felt my anxiety building and soon was realizing my natural peacefulness, fun and adventure climbing was vanishing. My internal Guidance system was sounding the alarm and I wasn't paying attention. Was I in fact attracting the danger?

Another signal was the lack of other hikers on the trail. Yes, it was a Sunday and while many had hiked the northern direction, it was strange given the popular summer route. Did they know something we didn't? What information did they have? The circumstantial evidence of skies, humidity, windspeed and direction were not independently alarming, but all together, they were. How did I miss the signals?

This was not a case of bravado and denial to simply push past it thinking we were faster and smarter. No, this was a series of small decisions compounded to result in a really bad day.

We need to slow our minds and focus on the static moments in time, the infinitesmal gap between the past and the future, the NOW so that we can see, hear, feel. and know where we are and if we are in alignment with our Desire.

We pressed on and as we came to the area near the base of the Mt. Jefferson summit cone, known as the Gap, we realized and knew there were limited choices to bail off the ridge from here on to Washington.

The winds were now gusting well into the 50+mph range and temps were dropping. The skies to the west were darker now and we could hear some thunder in the distance. The safer bail-out routes were to the west. The easterly direction had a few trails, none of which were recommended for descent, and certainly not in bad weather.

We felt a better decision was to continue south and to shelter at another high-mountain hut known as Lake of the Clouds. This would soon prove to be another flawed decision.

As we hiked through a remaining snow field, the winds were really gusting aggressively and the rain was constant. We were in our full rain and wind protection and it was harder to hear each other in the howling wind. The conditions were perfect for hypothermia now, wet, perspiring, temps dipping from the 70's to the lower 50's and into the 40's and fast.

I was concerned about Mo as she was struggling to keep pace against the constant high wind. We now could hear thunder to our south, precisely the direction of our travel! We had limited choices now and the visibility was fast deteriorating with more fog settling in. We could barely see the top of the Presidential summits and the intimidating massive Mt. Washington would only provide an occasional glimpse at its majestic peak.

We were both really struggling to walk as the wind gusts were now 60 to 80 mph and frequent. The thunder claps and lightning flashes were close in time, letting us know they were heading toward us. Above the tree line, we were the tallest organic matter standing! Lightning always seeks the path of least resistance.

At this point I tried to stay focused on getting us to shelter. My mind was headed to the place of how this had happened. How did I allow us to be in this precarious position?

We stopped and it took all but screaming to communicate with each other over the wind and loud thunder percussion. We still had well over a mile and half to go to reach the hut and the trail headed westerly around the summit cone. I didn't think we could get there, as the visibility was down to ten feet at times.

The antenna for the weather station on top of Washington was only visible for an instant and then faded into the fog and clouds. It was raining torrentially with intermittent hail. I told Mo our best chance to reach shelter was in fact to climb up to the summit and get to the Ranger station.

Yes, it seemed and felt counter intuitive but it was the shorter route to safety. We did all we could to manage a step at a time as the winds were now steady, well above 70 mph. I looked at my thermometer clipped to my outer shell jacket and the temperature had plunged into the 30's!

We made it approximately a quarter mile from the summit but the fog had completely engulfed it with very few glimpses of the antenna. It was our navigation beacon at this point. Mo could no longer walk into the wind. The Headwall into the Great Gulf Wilderness was on our eastern left side with an open relatively flat area to our right. No sign of shelter, no boulders or overhangs.

The intervals between thunderclaps were diminishing rapidly. We realized a thunder cell was likely coming straight at us. We pulled out a tarp, removed our packs and anything metallic and moved them several feet away. We crouched low to the ground desperately trying to hold the tarp over our heads.

We were being pummeled with hail the size of golf balls, tremendous rain, near freezing temps with thunder and associated lightning occurring virtually simultaneously! This was one of the few times in my life I questioned if I and we would survive.

• • • •

(KONA)

Mountain Man and Mom D were in a tough place. How different would it have been if I were already there? If he had learned some of the lessons. The trail ambassador would have shown him an alternative. He would learn the importance of being present in the moment. Maybe this wonderful human would have integrated the messages and made different decisions.

• • • •

(JOE)

As we sat there, I told my wife how sorry I was for allowing us to get in this position. It was surreal, it was summer and, in an instant, felt like winter. Sun turned to darkness, calm to violent wind, rain, hail, thunder, and lightning. An incredible storm. It is that way in life.

It is hard to be sure, but after about ten minutes under the tarp, with coincident thunder and lightning we heard an ear-blistering blast, at the same time feeling like someone had just kicked me in the chest while I had my finger in a light socket.

We were thrown forward and outside the feeble tarp protection. Mo and I felt a charge of electricity run through our bodies. Struck by lightning? How could it be we are still here? We both had no saliva left in our mouths. We grabbed the tarp and covered ourselves as best we could. We were both shaking and confused. We were alive! We had been right inside a thunder cloud.

Mo had tingling still running down her arms and my heart was racing. We had no choice but to wait it out and after about 45 minutes the rain and wind began to subside. We gathered ourselves and our gear and made our way on a compass heading and following the closely spaced cairns marking the trail, to the summit Ranger station, now fully engulfed in fog.

As we finally arrived we broke out in tears. The Rangers brought us inside and told us they had seen us coming over the ridge but given the conditions, could not send anyone out to help us. We said little to each other for a while, focused on getting into drier and warm clothes.

We eventually regained our composure and with self-reflection felt an awesome sense of gratitude. That had to be the closest I had come to consciously thinking and aware that I might die, and worse felt responsible for endangering my wife's life. **It is in the moment of decision that our destiny is formed.**

The storms passed completely after a couple of hours, leaving the summit engulfed in thick fog. It was eerily quiet outside now. We had about an hour hike down to the Lake of The Clouds hut where we were able to spend the night. After discussing and reviewing the radar with the Ranger, we were confident there were no more storms.

The weather station wasn't really equipped for overnight hikers except in an emergency. It certainly was one earlier when we were stranded. We made our way through the soupy fog and eventually arrived at the hut. The place was packed with an overabundance of hikers who were also caught in the storms albeit most had been below the exposed ridge line.

The Hut master was shocked to learn we had started the day at Madison and made it. We shared our story with him and others, mostly to help understand how this could happen, despite the prep work and experience.

I ended up writing several pages in the hiker's journal of the processional effect of small decisions and not paying attention to my internal guidance. We learned the actual latest weather report had never made it to the Hut master at Madison. At 5:45 that morning, the report actually called for rapidly worsening weather above the tree line with violent storms expected in the afternoon and discouraging any above-the-tree line hiking!

We also learned what we experienced was a "lighting splash." Effectively it can travel across the ground for miles and strike any organic matter in its way. As in life, when we are hard charging, not grounded and expecting the external world to be our only navigation, we can lose ourselves.

We slept well that night, save for some continued tingling we both were experiencing from the lightning. We hiked down the following day without incident and as one might imagine talked about it for a long time. God was there for us, we were sure. Little did I know, Kona would be showing up in a matter of months!

CHAPTER 11

Reflections

(KONA)

The casual person does not see or understand the incredible impact, the lack of coincidence, the uncanny ability of God, the Universe, Jesus, first through this man's mother, then through others, and mostly now through me, Kona.

The ultimate beautiful clear pond, still, and reflecting with perfection. Reflection without a ripple, with the ability for him to see himself in a way that no other person could understand. To uncover the masking of how special he really is. To see how a mission-driven Kona could make him smile, feel so full; no matter the circumstances, there is beauty in it for all to see. I am always there loving, wanting to show and share affection to the man. I am his spiritual friend and cosmic guide.

Does Joe, the Mountain Man know that he too is called to be a partner to me, a partner not to just a dog, but to the Highest Authority over the Universe … a Partner to God. To the Divine who too was at one time alone, lonely and scared. He had no one, nothing to share, to enjoy, to experience His Love. So yes, we were created out of His need for love.

At times, I wonder if these humans can detach from the level of distraction, spirits, now driven more by their humanness and disconnect from the natural order, having somewhat lost their way.

Some humans might suggest, this is too heavy, too deep, not so much fun. Why then look up at the stars, the sky, and ponder. Isn't it easier to just keep their heads down and burrow through every day, the "grind," as some call it? They fight against each other, compete for love, Time and things. They want it all now! **What is it they really want? Self love, worthiness, appreciation.**

How long will Joe "chase" it? How long has God wanted to experience it in return? How then is he and I supposed to move this forward? How do I help Joe, and through him, others achieve their highest and best?

● ● ● ●

(JOE)

Here is in part, how Kona changed me. I love that dog from such a deep, deep place in my heart and soul. It is an indescribable feeling. I would do anything for him. Is that what I would do for others? Really? Or does the behavior, events, and the humanness of others, that may not connect with me, block and impact my love?

I experience and mirror unconditional love back to Kona ... back to God? Where is the innocence in other "humans"? Where/how do we look past the judgment and see them for who they really are at the core?

It may not be as simple as it is with an innocent, playful, and wonderful Kona. True, he doesn't have the same distractions that might affect me. Just keep looking, and in the end, the longer I live, and experience, the more questions I ask. The more that life delivers -- the good, the bad, the ugly, the wonderful -- can and will affect us.

How much do our worldly possessions affect us, block us from the purity of nature? How many of us will pass through this phase of life evolution with a hollow mission, lack of true self-awareness and experience of allowing not only ourselves but others to just be who they really are?

Am I, are we, willing to look deeper, yes swim below the muck, through the darkness in the pond water to find the nutrient rich areas that feed the fish and creations?

To realize this is about looking inside me, inside you now, to not look away from that mirror, to not allow yourself to see only those areas that lack perfection, those parts that you deem matter, that "hair on the couch" doesn't matter.

Conversely, having made major changes to my body for the betterment of my soul, to allow me to better care for me, for others and give my love to so many, also allows a new level of vanity on which to focus? Ah, yes, it is a paradox.

Do we look away from the fat person, feeling deprived of love, angry at God for stealing away his father, watching his mother and siblings endure years and years of pain, so we somehow think, feel and believe we are unworthy. Somehow we did something wrong. Somehow being human is not okay, lacking the perfection of divinity is not okay, we tell ourselves, I told myself. No! How can I accept that?

Or do we look at ourselves, look at myself, and love and appreciate my body, my mind, the hard work to make the physical changes. Yes, no longer the "fat" kid, now the lean and muscular strong man, with higher levels of confidence. All would be good then, right?

Yes, on balance, or have I, have we, now let this positive improvement become in its own way a distraction, to now let the ego be in charge? In some ways to even think, feel, act as maybe God-like superior where it doesn't matter, we don't need anything or anyone or maybe even God? Can this be in my life or yours? It merits some time and reflection.

When I ponder these thoughts, I turn to Kona. Yeah, he is a dog, dammit, and allow the mirror to tell me, stay grounded, big guy. I am here for you no matter what has happened or will happen. You just need to decide to Trust, trust now and forever.

The events and experiences are all manifestations to help get closer to a level of enlightenment, to allow us to passionately love at an extraordinary level. ***Through love all is really possible!***

Kona and I are energetically connected. The connection is not by accident or coincidence. It is also me connecting with me!

CHAPTER 12

The Conduit

(JOE)

There were many times we would have parties at our house or at our daughter's place. She has three fur babies and we have two. Of course, the wonderful and special Kona and the adopted Enzo. Enzo, a black lab-shepherd mix, also came from the Midwest when we lived in the St Louis area.

He and Kona would grow to be as close as any two brother siblings could conceivably be. Enzo was mostly black with white on his belly and chin. He was a little guy when we adopted him at eleven weeks old and weighs in at around seventy-pounds now that he is grown. Kona, muscular and stout, tips the scales around twenty-three pounds. He has had a few excursions to twenty-five pounds, that Pug portion can chunk up if he is not exercising regularly.

He is very fast and agile due to the Jack in him. One might think Enzo would have his way with the little guy. Kona, like many of the smaller breeds, sees himself very differently in a reflection in a pond or mirror. He sees this large, powerful, confident, courageous creature. I'm convinced he sees a lion! How do you see yourself?

He stands up to anyone and anything. When playing with Enzo, he uses his strong hind legs to drive and maneuver the big guy, catch him off balance and make a wrestling type move, reach under, grab the opposite leg and flip Enzo on his back, then pin him! You think he was watching the WWF!

They are a real blast to watch along with their cousins, Jenna's dogs. Her oldest, Tiki, complemented with Wally and Bruschi, get along very well and love to play together. Bruschi was the runt of the litter and is a small little Boston terrier, with an attitude. He is black and white with a head too big for his body, not just physically. Wally, like Tiki, is a Bug (Boston and Pug mix) and is brindle colored, super high strung, bouncy, nervous with a somewhat typical youngest child-wanting-to-fit-into-the-pack syndrome.

Jenna's place had a few acres surrounded with trees and unfenced. Typically, our boys would stay close to the boundaries but at times, bolt off into the woods, creating anxiety for us to have to search for them. They ultimately would return, muddy from digging and playing, lost in their own world of being dogs. Life does go on, damn it!

It is okay, things usually turn out fine is how we were taught growing up. Worry is simply faith misplaced. It is a great belief to live by, although not always as easy as it sounds. We all face moments of challenge. We worry about our kids, our family, friends, and loved ones.

One day at Jenna's, our boys took off into the woods, no doubt chasing some creature or just conditioned to play and explore. This day would be different. They did not return in the typical amount of time despite our frantic calling for them.

I realized this particular day that my love for Kona was well beyond what most people would consider normal, and outside of what I would have considered "normal." I was beyond worried and desperately trying to remain calm and keep myself from thinking the worst had occurred. You know, hit by a car, another larger animal, or a pack of coyotes may have attacked. **The mind can run wild, oh ye of little faith.**

After taking all the necessary actions of posting a missing-dogs report on social media and calling local authorities, we continued searching. I literally ran through the woods for hours screaming their names but to no avail. We drove around doing the same and were now becoming very worried.

Strangely, I also started to wonder what was really going on with me. Was this really about the dogs, acutely more about Kona than Enzo? Yes, I was concerned about Enzo, but not the same as Kona. What did Kona represent? Why was I so scared for him? Why was I deeply pleading for him to be okay and come back?

There was more than just "hair-on-the-couch doesn't matter" going on here. Was it love? Or fear looking in at me, capturing me and engulfing me totally. Could it be? Was Kona truly partly a reflection, that if he was gone, I would be lost again? That the missing gap, starting to close, would return? The possibility of living more and more in the moment and appreciating the gift as the driveway for its simple reality would too vanish? Alternatively, could it be it was just because he was a fun and cool dog? I think NOT!

Hours passed and Enzo finally returned, all muddy and dirty, exhausted and thirsty but with no sign of Kona. It would soon be dark and my worry quotient was increasing dramatically. I had to find this dog. Ultimately, after almost losing hope (where else does that show up in your life?), what had occurred is he was digging around a large shed on a property about a mile away.

During our earlier search, we had approached the owner and inquired if he had seen the boys. He said he had seen a dog matching Kona's description out behind his house. Fortunately, Jenna decided to go back to that property and thought she heard Kona crying.

● ● ● ●

(KONA)

So here I was in this tight space, unable to move forward or backward. I'm supposed to be the agile one, Kona, the trail ambassador, how do I find myself here? Interestingly, in this dog form, humans assume we are always living in the moment with no sense of past or future time.

Today, under this dark cold building, and physically stuck, I was frantically digging with my paws and my snoot. I was thirsty from the dirt and mud inside my mouth. My nails were packed with earth making it more difficult to scrape and attempt to find a way out.

In those moments, I began to understand and "feel" the emotion of fear and a sense of time crept in. My dog instincts were being mixed with, what, human emotion? I noticed it was getting darker and colder. I was experiencing fear! I am a "Southie (a Southie is an irish-american human from South Boston)," how can that be? On top I am a dog, on a mission. How can this be happening? I wondered. Here I was scared, trapped and feeling abandoned. Would Mountain Man find me? Was he looking for me? Did I matter? Did he realize he was also on a mission?

As time went on, my eyes began to water, my nose, typically wet, was now dry. I had no saliva left and my mouth was sore and riddled with a horrible taste of earth, rich with the scents of numerous organisms. My keen senses of taste and smell remained and I could taste my own fear and pondered if I would see Joe, pack leader, again? Would we play, go on those walks and crazy hikes? Who would help him navigate the path? How and who would finish my mission if I would transform back to another energy form?

• • • •

(JOE)

In his exploring and perhaps chasing something, he got himself trapped in an area under the shed and could not back himself out. Jenna and the property owner were able to dig him out and other than being dirty, tired and dehydrated, he was okay! Well, I was not, and you would think I had lost my first-born child. It emphasized to me and others, that there was more going on here than meets the eye.

I started to wonder how I will react when Kona passes on, which should be well before I do. I dread that thought more than anyone can imagine. It brings to me a sense of mortality at another level. Is it really about Kona's mortality? Sure it is, to a point.

The bigger issue though, is about the lessons of love, self-love, unconditional self-love, living in the present and ultimately my own personal mortality.

Where do we go really? Where will Kona go? Will I see him? Will I see God? Does God want to see me? Does God love me? How could He not? Does God think I love Him? Can I love Him if I don't love me? Do I know he needs it too? Is HE lonely? **Kona is here to make it clear and to carry the signals back and forth.**

I have always, as many of us do, want to remain young forever. I do work to take care of my mind, body and soul but the reality is time, in the place of what I hope and pray is eternal life, is not on our side. So, what then do we do, what then do I do? What does Kona do? Age with grace, do more now, why wait? Get on with it, live with passion, stop fretting about what others think and expect. Leave their model of the world for them, sans judgment. Your, my, model of the world, how you see things is yours and yours only.

So here was this little dog, out playing and exploring, being true to himself, and getting wedged under a shed, relatively fine, and yet there are deeper meanings to the resulting experience.

It is important to look at what is going on in your life and evaluate your reactions to situations. Look for why and how you react and what it might represent. This event was an opportunity to face my own fears, the fear of being unloved and unworthy. Come on now, I was just worried about the little dog! Why do I crave love so much and find myself chasing opportunities, chasing affection, wanting to be needed? Yes, the popular-boy syndrome. Hard wired like Kona, chasing the squirrels.

Whatever has occurred in your life there is always a choice on how to evaluate its meaning. It is up to you to assign what it means to you. It is not for others to decide. You get to choose it as an excuse, or to use it as empowering leverage to drive yourself higher in whatever that means for you: success, to experience joy and gratitude, ultimately feel worthy and more than adequate, to realize you and we are here by Divine Guidance, that energy cannot be destroyed only transformed. That we are all somehow interconnected, that the cells in our body are all individual energy power-plants communicating with each other on the status of our health.

Kona is my spiritual partner and guide; what and who is yours? There are angels for all of us, spiritual help from loved ones, that we can draw in. It is about remaining open and in touch with how we really feel rather than working to manage our thoughts. There really are no coincidences in this life. We are energy with magnetic forces that can marshal the Universe to bring into our lives all that we focus on. Yes, like attracts like and if you examine your life you will find this to be true.

Whether it is as simple as wondering why when we are hurried, anxious, and late for an appointment we seem to hit every red light or looking back at a more significant and profound accomplishment.

Think back, how were you feeling when you focused on something you really wanted, and what did you believe? Confident and feeling positively sure it would happen? We all experience fear. It is okay to feel fear. It is in the end though, simply false-evidence of altered-reality. Allowing ourselves to engage with it vs. denying or suppressing it is important.

CHAPTER 13

The Falls

(KONA)

It was an early adventure in New Hampshire when I was probably four that I gained the distinguished title as "trail ambassador." We were up in an area where there are many of these large old things called mountains, the White Mountains. Forty-eight of which were over four thousand feet high and were of keen interest to my pack leader. He and his human partner, (wife) Mo, or Mom D or Mrs. D as some call her, love to climb them. Maybe they get a treat when done, I don't know.

What I do know is it is hard work for humans and canines alike, even though I feel and experience the beauty of the streams, rivers, the leaves blowing, the amazing backset of a blue sky, the millions of various smells, the ability to sniff and pee without hesitation or limitation.

I remember my very first 4000-footer. It was a winter day with lots of the white stuff called snow on the ground and the trails were glistening and sparkling. The sun was shining and the winds were calm. Mountain Man and Mrs. D seemed all excited about my first climb and as they call it, peak-bagging. How did I know? Well, they did the squeezing thing as we prepared to climb up the mountain.

I was young, but they seemed to recognize I was really built to navigate the trails and really didn't need to be on that cord-like device called a leash. It makes us feel trapped and affects our behaviors.

The trail itself was smooth and slippery for the humans and even for me despite my great paws and nails. We made it to the top and celebrated. They seemed really happy and me, well I was having fun just being out, running, playing with whatever I could dig up in the packed powder.

The way down was a different experience. Since it was "icy," the pack leader sat down and was sliding down fast. They were having fun. It is interesting watching these creatures who manage to walk and run on only two legs, actually sit on their rear quarters and move fast. I would start to run, then tuck my nails in and slide like my pack leaders. It was as they would say, fun and exhilarating. I was happy to be back in the car and was fast asleep on our ride home.

Then there was another time, one very cold day we were out to go to a place called Bridal Veil Falls, which is a place they would go often for what was referred to as a "day hike." It sounds like a walk to us dogs.

It was bitterly cold that day even for this area of New Hampshire and pack leader was really feeling energized and passionate about the trip. In doing so, he was well prepared with all the necessary emergency items should we get into trouble. Hiking in the mountains for even a day in those conditions could lead to trouble.

After they got all dressed in their "mountain gear," on went my winter coat. A fluorescent green thing, it was a bit suffocating on my body but it was important to protect me. It was about 10 degrees when we started with a light but steady wind. New fallen snow was fresh and deep. Pack leader Joe and Mo donned these funny looking paddles that go on their paws, I mean their feet, called snow shoes. They help them distribute their weight and stay mostly on top of the snow.

My paws can get cold and icy between the toes which is painful and can be dangerous, so they tried these funny bootie things. Hey, is anyone paying attention, I'm a dog! I hated them and refused to wear them. Once in a while, Joe would put some jelly *like stuff on the bottom of my paws to help insulate and protect them from getting raw.*

As we moved through the snow, it was a challenge to keep up with him. I usually take the lead but not today, not in the bitter cold and deep snow. It was exhausting.

I was right on the heels of his snowshoes, and we were moving in a synchronized fashion. Right, left, right, left we just kept climbing. It was like a melody, the sounds of the snow coming off this powerful human's large feet. It was rhythmic, it was almost trance-like, the fast moving wind in the background, his breath and mine in parallel, my head moving left and right as the snow came off his heels and into my face.

I could sense the connection Joe had with me that day. It was surreal and time seemed to standstill. The sense of purpose right then, the mission, the desire for love, the knowing we were all here for a reason, the sense and curiosity of what God wanted and needed. I also wondered was God lonely? Did He need love? the presence of the Almighty, right there, **"Where two or three are gathered together in My name, I am there in the midst of them"** (Matthew 18:19-20)

It was getting increasingly colder now and Joe was so focused and deliberate in his movement, I wasn't sure if he realized what was happening. My core temperature was dropping, given my small size, belly being close to the ground, and the falling snow. The snow trails coming off his snowshoes were getting trapped between my tummy and god-awful green coat, creating a mechanism to pull even more body heat away from me.

As we approached close to the top near the Falls, the wind had become fierce. My pack mom got Joe's attention as she thought I was in trouble. I was in trouble! I was now shivering uncontrollably, my paws were ice embedded, and I was in pain. I didn't want to do the barking thing or make an issue. I too, was focused.

Once the Mountain Man realized what was happening, he unselfishly picked me up; I could feel both his nervousness and his love, his caring, the way he looked into my eyes at that moment, his assessment of the situation and the growing concern. He removed my coat, only long enough to remove the ice that was stuck to my belly, and started running down the mountain. He knew he had to get me to a warmer place and fast.

I will remember that day, when I knew as much as I was on a mission for him, he was on one for me, too! The love I started to see and feel was growing more and more and was so much greater than when I arrived on that anxiety-ridden, long cold flight from my Kansas home. So, you see, the long and more complex transformation of an already compassionate human was well under way now. Amazingly, two experiences in the mountains, seemingly started with similar expectations, ended so differently.

Fortunately, that day he was able to get me, this little beast of a dog, back to the car swiftly before my body temperature dropped to very dangerous levels. Here was an example of when he realized how much he loved and cared for me, a being who was so much more than a dog. The whole concept of unconditional love, certainly for one human, was becoming possible, no matter what the circumstance. Knowing this intellectually is only part of experiencing it with all their hearts, mind, body and Spirit.

CHAPTER 14

Transition

(JOE)

There was that horrible cold winter night at a concert in New York City (maybe like the night Kona left Kansas), the not feeling well with a bad cold, the experimenting with drugs, the partying, the confused teenager wanting to change his life but stuck in a pattern that misaligned with his true Desire. What then should I do?

So that night, through the fear and pain of a terrible experience, when I lost myself and felt like I was in a different universe and belief that it was permanent, that I would never return to a feeling of normalcy, was terrifying. That quiet, oh so quiet conventional talk with my mom where she first sat and just listened to my attempt at small talk.

She didn't react with her typical Italian tough-mother discipline. You know, a bit of yelling, a wooden spoon crack on the arm or butt. I was afraid and just needed her to listen. I could tell she knew something was wrong at a deeper level.

I felt bad, incongruent, shameful for my behaviors. I was disappointing my mother, who already had her hands more than full with my dad's situation.

I don't remember what we spoke about other than she seemed uncharacteristically tolerant and understanding. She told me several stories from her childhood, days at the convent, examples of how God interceded in her life and those of others. The miracles she saw take place. I mean here it was around four in the morning, I had been out all night and likely seemed disheveled, to say the least.

It was getting late and reluctantly I went to bed. I could taste the fear, the feeling of failure. I lay there and was truly frightened. How do I get out of this? How could this be happening? I remembered mom's words "never leave Jesus."

I prayed as best as I could manage but then asked Him with passion conviction and clarity, if HE would just get me out of this, I promised I would change my life, start doing the right stuff, get focused on taking care of myself and make my mother and Him proud of me. I would get on and do the work.

What work, I wasn't quite sure, but His work, the words from the late-night discussions with mom echoed through my head.

This night, this event where through some poor decisions to put things in my body that were not good for me, combined with already being ill from a bad winter cold, distorted my reality. It was like being in a different dimension, looking through a portal back to the physical reality surrounding me. My connection to all that I knew was broken. I felt abandoned, with no control.

The lack of congruency I felt at the time had been building. I was in conflict with my core values, and more importantly with my alignment to my deeper calling and desire.

Mom must have known it. I am convinced know looking back she absolutely was connected and was in on the life lesson. I can remember the date and time of the event, the smell of the air at the concert and in the subway, the face of the token cashier, his voice, the waiting for the train, the incredible feeling of despair and uncertainty, feeling lost having crossed a line, wondering ultimately if I would ever feel "normal" again. Ask and you shall receive. Well, boy did I ask that night. I begged God.

My life did start to change immediately. Long-lasting results sure took some time, but it clearly was an inflection point and my life trajectory definitely changed.

Who would've thought that night that the processional effect of that ASK would lead to a highly successful career in the aerospace and business world. Many might discount this example of a typical teenager who hadn't yet grown up and would have eventually figured it out. There are many stories where this is not the case.

As you look back and examine your life, where are your inflection points? When did you ask and were blessed with an answer, perhaps in a different form from what you expected?

I did have a passion for growing personally and learning more about the more spiritual, non-physical aspects of life. I remember being in that high school psychology class and just loving the subject. Wow. I thought, here is a way to understand why people behave and do what they do.

I didn't have much guidance on college selection, or course of study. Mom pushed hard for excellence and knew school was important, but she was unable to provide specific direction. I didn't know then how I could make a good living in the psychology area, and while I loved the subject, I knew I was good at math and science.

I did find airplanes intriguing as the flight path into La Guardia was visible outside our apartment windows. I found these machines that could fly fascinating; my career in aerospace probably was born there.

I was curious about energy, not just from the physics view, but from a metaphysical perspective. How did it work in us? I loved, and still love, looking into the night sky and wondering in amazement at the stars and universe. How many of us have become too busy and consumed to do that?

I recall being on a bus in New York City watching thousands of people going about in what seemed like a purely robotic manner. Do they wonder, I wondered? Why are we here, what are we supposed to be doing?

Have we lost connection with the Universe, God, Spirit, whatever you call it? It is not a question about religion but about love and connection to a Higher Power. It is amazing to look back now and see where and when this all germinated in me!

There was this insatiable desire, a real craving to know what the hell really matters. My father, by work standards and job description, was a porter and union worker for the New York City Transit Authority. He had six brothers and sisters and was the oldest. He married very late in life, even by today's standards. He was the patriarch of his family after his parents passed.

He was ahead of his time regarding exercise and sport. He worked out at the YMCA and other gyms, more like a professional athlete of the era. I had such a limited time with him, I never really grew to know him. He was a conservative and a risk-averse individual.

My mom wanted to get us out of the Bronx and buy this little house on Long Island but Pop just wasn't comfortable with a mortgage. He did like to travel and see places, however, because he ended up going back to Italy and marrying my mother.

It wasn't a technically arranged marriage, but here was my mom living in a convent in her thirties and through friends of families, they were connected. My mom was encouraged to marry him, start a family and go live in the U.S. for a "better" life.

My father was also an amazing artist. He sculpted, painted, carved beautiful pieces. Some of his work was astonishing. My dad was a Pisces and they love harmony. I believe he found much of it through his art. I wanted to know, would this creativity show up in my life? How, where, and why would it show up? Would it show up at all? Does it matter? Would I know? Would others see it?

CHAPTER 15

Mirror Mirror on the Wall

(KONA)

Humans, (and all forms of Spirit) need love and support, starting with themselves first. **It is that first time you can stand in the privacy of your own space, in front of a mirror and look deeply into your own eyes, that portal to your own soul, and stare for minutes where time seems to disappear; and ultimately say "I love you" to you!**

This is one of the greatest gifts you and we all deserve. It is with and through love all else can be managed. When Joe looks deeply into my eyes, I can see that gaze and know he is, in some strange way, looking back at himself, wanting so much of what I, Kona, do naturally.

In 2014, I watched as they came to pack up the truck with all the family stuff. Looks like we were on the move again. Mountain Man was now setting off to lead some new company back out in the Midwest in a larger-than-life job!

I wondered if this was right for him. He wanted to do something so different, so much more in line with his passion for people. He had a real love for fitness, nutrition, and coaching others.

I sat and observed him pull back from making the ultimate break and perhaps yield to the relative comfort and perceived security of what he knew and did well. How would the gap close? Was he stuck -- and I was here to help him? What was I to do? I could keep being me; you know, the wild sparky trail ambassador and just be there for him.

He continued to bond closer to me to the point where he would talk to me about his decisions, fears, what he wanted, and didn't want. I could only read his energy. We canines have evolved quite a bit but cannot lip read human partners!

It was after about two years, he seemed to be traveling most of the time, but seemed to be in his element, when a serious calling for me to be there for him would show up. Time for me, time for God to be there.

We lived in this big house with a hilly back yard out in St. Charles County, Missouri. Enzo and I would go to the dog park to get some play time with our friends, especially Nikko. Nikko was this cool little white Scottish terrier, a new pack pal Enzo and I met there frequently.

We would have a wonderful time, as there was a pond with what people call a dive dock. Not me, as us Pug-ish body types are fine with water up to our belly but not much for the swimming thing. I know, I am a dog and dogs are supposed to all know how to swim. I sort of slap my front paws splashing as I try hard to keep my head above the water. I get it done but not pretty to watch! Enzo, on the other hand, loves the water. He has those great webbed Labrador paws designed for swimming.

Many of my canine colleagues would love to get a full run up on the dock and then launch themselves to attempt to catch a flying thing these humans would throw called a frisbee. Seemed like a lot of work and then they would swim back to the shore.

One day I was walking on the dock and as I peered over into the water to chase a reflection, I lost my balance and fell into the muddy dark pond water, almost going under the dock. That could have been a bad day. Fortunately, Joe was there, and he reached down into the muck and immediately pulled me out of the water. **Wow, we are always there for each other.**

Later that year, Joe lost his beloved mother, whom he cherished, as he appreciated all she did to help him and his siblings, including getting a great education, despite the challenges they faced. At the same time, momma pack leader lost her very close uncle.

It was a challenge for them both. I believe this was a pivotal point for my Mountain Man, pack leader extraordinaire.

He was somewhat relieved now that his mom wasn't suffering, and he just knew she had to be in a great place, a place where all was pure, full of love, expansive, without limitation. Did he know that? He certainly wanted now, more than ever, to believe it.

Was I starting to really help him see and experience it? Did he have a clue about what was really going on? And yet, he was also starting to feel a sense of guilt and wanting to be closer to his family again. His son and daughter and little grandson all lived back in the Northeast. He was conflicted as he was enjoying his "job" for the most part; it seemed we would remain out here in Missouri for quite some time.

There are many attributes about us dogs that are important to understand. We connect and learn about each other differently than our human counterparts do. We spend time by using our incredible sense of smell to determine many things.

We don't understand how humans simply walk up to each other and sometimes touch paws or as they say, shake hands. How do they know if they are compatible and can trust the other to not attack? We four-legged wonders are more prescriptive and usually pragmatic. We do the sniff test and that starts from a distance and progresses to a direct nose-to-rear test.

It is through this process we make an initial assessment. Is there a threat, can we walk together, play together? How will we proceed? Yes, humans look at us funny as we do them. If you watch us in a pack, we use the method to determine the pecking order; size does not matter. We need to know where we stand in the pack. We operate based on a set of rules that are understood by all.

I, being a terrier type, am hard-wired to chase. It is about the chase, of creatures like squirrels or chipmunks. I see or smell one and a full-blown chase is on. I lose myself in it! It is not so much about conquering, but more about the variety of it all, the sense of new and different.

And as it is with Joe my pack leader. He loves variety and the thrill of it all. As the saying goes, like a dog who chases the pickup truck, catches it and doesn't know what to do! Does Joe know what and why he is in chase mode? I will keep on him. This is an area that is a challenge for me due to my wiring. Joe, the Mountain Man and I share this trait!

CHAPTER 16

Hair Doesn't Matter

(JOE)

Love has no limits, no boundaries, no judgment. Real men love and can show love. It is okay and necessary to feel and express emotion. We are often conditioned to hold it back, to be the tough guy. To be "manly," to be strong, to show emotion can be perceived as weakness.

The hunter must not show fear or love, it is the pecking order, right. Men also have feminine energy. Women also have masculine energy. It is the yin and yang, the tension in the spring, the balancing forces that drive equilibrium in us, in all things, in the Universe. When men engage with their feminine energy (not femininity) it is a beautiful aspect of our spiritual makeup.

We are not simply hard-charging alpha males, we are in fact driven by the same needs as women. Being unloved and unworthy are our two greatest fears. These can take root and shape our behaviors and even our identity. Allow yourself the gift of love, especially starting with love of self; it then can flow to others without boundary.

What beliefs do we hold for ourselves? What beliefs do we hold about others individually or globally? Do these beliefs serve us and allow us to be authentic? Beliefs are either strong or weak based on a reference system of life experiences. Much like the legs of a table, beliefs can be strong and solid and plentiful to hold up that tableop up -- beliefs can be empowering or not.

Why then is it easier to identify with, express, and hold onto disempowering beliefs? Think about it: if we had real self-love and felt it we might in fact find it easier to express it with confidence, why don't we hold more positive beliefs? So then, the challenge would be to break down and replace the disempowering beliefs, by adding new references, new table legs.

What are some things you and I can do to establish a more positive belief? What if the challenge question is do you love? If so, what if the real question is do you love you? Is there hesitation? Is there doubt and confusion? What if the response is no? What then? Does it draw fear and wonderment? Or is it easier to walk away from the question? Is it easier to be less than you at the amazing deserving being of your core?

Yes, it might seem so at the surface but then what will be missed? What has been missed and wasted already? Why not ask instead for references that can help establish self love, worthiness?

• • • •

I always enjoyed cars since I was a kid; back in 2001 I had purchased this special BMW. It was sort of a prize possession. I worked hard to obtain it, enjoyed it immensely and always kept it cleaned and polished.

I was certainly growing more and more affection for Kona, but dogs in my car, not a chance. Hair, nails on the leather, "schmooze" on the windows, I was not having it. Seems like a reasonable expectation to most, and it is on the surface.

The deeper question to ask, though, is what is below the surface? What value have I truly placed on the car, where does it end up, where else does it show up in your life?

Kona was a clear lens helping me start seeing the distractions, the areas I overvalued that were blocking me from being me, from letting go of so much of the past that was showing up through these nonsensical priorities and concerns.

It was a busy morning and Mo and I needed to leave for work. This would've been a typical morning except she had to leave much earlier, before the puppy day-care was open. I remember telling her to just go, and not to worry, that I would get Kona there. I have to say she was a bit befuddled and asked me if I was going to call a taxi or how was I actually going to get him there? I simply said I am going to drop him off on my way to the office. She reacted with a "WHAT??"

The amazing thing, as I look back at it, it was a truly unabated, unconflicted response, no confusion, no second thoughts. How could it be, she wondered? What just happened to my husband?

Well, you know sometimes you just need to dance with the music. Let the flow of the rhythm carry you and not try to figure out every step and be sure it all works perfectly.

This seemingly simple and some would say shallow act, represented a marked change and the student was learning. I was ready: The Universe, God, Jesus in my life answered with a Spirit Guide who was sent to me through my desire asking, in the form of a dog, this wonderful, fun, happy, loving creature.

On a long journey, an airplane is constantly correcting its positioning. Slight changes in direction can substantially alter the destination. Just a few degrees off of a heading either deliberately or drifting without notice can dramatically affect where we arrive.

It is the same with us: who we become, what we believe, whose life we impact, how much success we have (or not,) if we are healthier or have more disease, are loved or are loving, are fearful or courageous.

Pay attention to the heading through your internal guidance system. How we feel and what meaning we assign to events is paramount.

It was clear now he was my Kona and we would be there for each other and as would soon become more evident, for God! You know what, I must say Kona really did enjoy the ride as well, sitting up so proud of himself. He knew what happened, and was not confused.

It can be said that the quality of one's life is proportional to the quality of the questions we ask, the level of openness we allow. There are many examples in life of seemingly minor "hang-ups" that represent much deeper limitations and blockages to be closer to the authentic you.

What was seemingly a simple and average expectation of wanting to maintain a clean house and car (there is nothing wrong with that unless its value is overstated) can have masking effects.

There is certainly nothing wrong with wanting things to be tidy and clean! I still keep my cars and house clean. It is more about the energy and value you place on it and what it represents. Is it your external concerns about what the world view might be? Are you driven and or worried about perception?

Is it worth looking for those areas in your life where you think "hair matters?" Kona and I are here to help you understand the search is worth it and that "hair doesn't matter!"

CHAPTER 17

Another Angel

(JOE)

One of the things I enjoy most is the sport of hiking and climbing mountains. I love to hike, to experience nature and adventure. There was a key figure in my life who made that appreciation and skillset possible. How does a city kid from the South Bronx end up with a deep passion, love, and skills for adventurous extended treks, including sleeping outdoors, and climbing mountains?

I was fortunate enough to have been a Boy Scout, but more importantly, blessed to have had a fantastic Scoutmaster named Fred. Fred was originally from Maine and was an English teacher but loved and believed in the power and teachings associated with

Scouting. It was through this process that I became educated and skilled at the various things one needed to become an accomplished outdoorsman.

I love to hike at any time but particularly in the solitude of winter. The freshly fallen snow, against a beautiful blue sky, the deep evergreen trees, the frozen bodies of water and waterfalls, all make it a magical experience. The environment of being close to nature is so good for the soul. It can be amazingly transformational in multiple ways. Take this inner-city kid who learned what appeared to be outdoor skills for just fun and vacation.

I grew to have courage beyond my imagination. Well beyond those early days of feeling inadequate, because I was fat, because I didn't have the typical daddy relationship, my lack of confidence -- although heavily -balanced by mom's love for me – gave me the belief that I could do anything I desired.

It is so easy for us in this life to walk by moments, that seem not significant, yet are so powerful if we just stop for a few minutes and be present. Kona has been an instrumental part of that journey for me.

I was a boy and young man who had no barometer, who only wanted to be more, not knowing how, to strive for excellence, to show that how you started is not relevant, that we all have the same amount of time available to us, that we are all passing through here. We can debate where we came from and where we are going, but not the fact we all will "die" from this form of life on earth.

Should there be a moment we contemplate worry? For us, one of the greatest of all Teachers, Jesus, said, "But about that day or hour no one knows, not even the angels in heaven, nor the Son, but only the Father" **Matthew 24: 36**

What is of utmost importance is that we don't become devoid of the simpler blessings: appreciating the morning sun on a lake, the gaze and wonderment of the stars in the sky, the cold raindrops on recently fallen autumn leaves, the sound of a child crying a first breath, the sound of a kid splashing in puddles and laughing in the playground, the sounds of birds singing in the woods, the wind blowing fiercely on a cold blustery winter night, the massive amounts of abundance God has provided all around us. We just need to stop and choose to look.

The real question is, what does it take to rest long enough to see, feel, and appreciate it rather than blindly walk through life with what we believe are our chores. No, the Divine One would want and expect us to have more.

So, it is for me in those days in the woods. Kona is so much a part of that lesson in humility. He is a loving, selfless creature who not only knows how to love but does so with reckless abandon.

He is a dog who appreciates the morning belly rubs, just because, who stops to have the sun rays overwhelm and drench him in warmth. Is it not as true for God? Does God not love us with reckless abandon? Unconditionally with no bounds. And what does He want and or need? Hmmmm…..

Yes, Kona is a fantastic Guide who by nature has mastered the definition of being in the moment. Do we stop to listen and learn from other species? Other spiritual beings having their own animal, albeit non-human, experience? Are they here just for our pleasure? Kona is arguably very human-like in many of his behaviors, and I suggest he is simply in flow and alignment with his partner and friend, having a clear mission and purpose.

When we get into it, I find I am looking into a mirror when I look at Kona. He is a pond reflecting back at me. He is in teaching mode all the time to let me know he is there. He watches my every move and knows and reads my energy. He can immediately assess my emotional state.

CHAPTER 18

Dance – Just Dance

(JOE)

The challenge we have is "like attracts like:" What we focus on we get. It doesn't matter if we want it or not. We just keep focusing on the end results and wonder how it happens, the way and the why? The Law of Attraction is at work, like a giant magnet. It will rally the forces of the entire universe; the people, places, and things.

It is about letting go and getting in touch with your true desire. We have magnetic energy. We draw to us what we really want, or what we really don't want!

Controlling thoughts every day is complex and would not be practical. However, "thoughts are things," so how do we manage them? It is easier to focus on how we feel, how we choose to interpret an experience, than to directly control the thousands of thoughts we have.

If and when we stay focused on being in a good emotional place, make the quiet time to get in touch with our internal guidance system, then we can know if we are in alignment with our true and ultimate Desire. It is not about making this super complex and mystical.

Find simple ways to feel good. Establish simple rules to feel positive emotions. It is a choice. Nothing has any meaning except for the meaning we assign to it.

I'll give you an example. I love to dance. Music can move me to a happy place fast. What is it for you? Let's take dancing. It is a great expression of the inner self. Anyone can dance, if they allow themselves to be free from perfection, not studying all the steps to get it just right. That feeling of clumsiness and stiffness. Just allow yourself to get into the flow of the rhythm and let yourself move as it feels to you.

Life is your dance, not anyone else's. Dancing can be so energizing and freeing. What holds many back from it? How will I look, what will others think, I'm not good enough, etc. Here is a fear of judgment of what others think about me. What if I commit to change my life and do something different?

Maybe it isn't dancing for you and that's okay, find what works to help you to spend time feeling good! Maybe it is a form of exercise, walking, hiking etc. What matters is an empowering activity, where you can get to a place of feeling good and then spend a few quiet minutes just being and focusing on your desires.

Many will say, well, you don't know my life, my challenges, what I endure and that's not fair. All of us have a variety of challenges and they certainly vary in magnitude and impact. We are magnetic fields of energy. It is also on a scale. It is about moving up the vibrational scale from perhaps feeling bad to feeling better.

It isn't magic, it's about progression and about allowing our internal and spiritual guidance system to do its work through emotion. How we feel correlates to what we attract and if we are aligned with our desire.

You see, what we all want to know is, am I really loved and am I worthy? Among humanity's greatest fear is this: Spiritual guidance, where is it? Many times, even when we receive it, we suppress it, we tuck it away, it is scary and we don't know what to do with it.

We choose to remain and swim on top of the pond rather than dive deeper into it and realize the abundance of what is down there. To take a deeper look into ourselves, into our own souls, to learn and love who we really are is to evolve and become more enlightened. To realize we are not an accident as the Universe (God) notices intent and doesn't make mistakes. To know that we are right where we are supposed to be regardless of the circumstances and even if doesn't feel like it.

It is through this process of openness about ourselves that we can become more fulfilled, to see a clearer picture of what and where we go next, to enjoy the bliss of a simple sunset and to be forever present in the moment.

CHAPTER 19

The Chase

(KONA)

Part of Joe's connection to me and alignment with why I was sent in this form was to teach him about the chase. He didn't see this at all at first; yet another blind-spot.

Here he is slowly learning and seeing so much, whether in the business world or any other environment. I LOVE the chase. He loves the chase. Like us dogs chasing the proverbial pick-up truck, this has been his story in part. He loves the variety and adventure it brings.

The reality is he and humans often also chase love and when they see it and want it for themselves, they don't know what to do with it. Rather than embrace it, they at times push it away.

Are Joe and other men afraid of self-love? It feels so good to love oneself first, as it leads to so much more love to give others. So why do so many find it hard to do and experience? Are they confused with it being a narcissistic trait they are not, or should not be proud of, or others would see it as purely self-serving? This is one area of the chase, so when you catch it, embrace it and hold on to it. Bring it into yourself and allow it to feel good.

It is Divine to experience self-love. Through this experience, resistance flows away, and the ability to grow increases in confidence and in faith, and an extraordinary celestial alignment with Desire occurs. Don't just think it -- feel it. Allow yourself to experience it.

You see, my message in part, was about the chase. That opened his eyes and helped him understand that at times of self-doubt and fear, love of self becomes vitally important to push through and know, at a deep level, that you can be whatever and whomever you desire, and accomplish anything you want and deserve. It casts away the vitriol of lashing out to the world, which is a cry for help that is misinterpreted by some if not most.

• • • •

(JOE)

Back in my grammar-school days, I remember mom pushing so hard on the importance of doing well in school. It was the message about possibility, the ability to have the world open up if we were accomplished in school. It was never okay to do "average" or even "good" work; a "97" on an exam could have and should have been "100."

In life, striving for excellence, truly outstanding performance becomes a discriminator, especially in today's world. It is no longer okay to do a good or even great job, be a good or great father, husband, teacher. The rewards are saved for those who are outstanding at what they do and strive/drive to maintain that level.

Think about it, kids today are normalized to think everyone is doing okay. Think about the participation trophies and no demarcation on report cards to suggest one may be below par, and others excelling. This may sound good until the reality begins to strike at college entry. More and more colleges are only accepting the "cream of the crop," the top performers. Those kids who thought all was fine and they were like the rest of the group, with the same opportunities. received a crushing blow when they were not accepted to college. There is value to the chase to achieve our highest and best, when we come from a place of love, self love first.

CHAPTER 20

The "Pole"

(JOE)

In 1998, during the Life Mastery portion of Mastery University, a ten-day sort of adult boot camp for adults in mastery of the physical world, covered physiology, exercise, strict adherence to a detoxing nutritional plan and a forty-foot, yes forty-foot fire walk!

There was one particular exercise, for me and for many, that was more of a psychological than physical challenge. It was to climb what was called a pamper pole. It is basically a telephone-like pole, over 50 feet above the ground. It is tapered and gets smaller in diameter as you move toward the top. It is designed and installed in the ground to have some inherent instability, so it moves around as you attempt to climb it. There are some rungs to use for foot holds and aids as you climb. They become more sparse and smaller in size as you ascend. So, what is this?

The objective is to climb to the top of this fifty-foot pole and then decide to either simply jump off (you are in a harness with a team member holding a rope on belay) or jump outward to attempt to grab a trapeze some twelve feet away. If you grab the trapeze, you would then let go and be slowly lowered on a belay.

Well here was a time where I froze in space. I knew about the "pole" and already had some anxiety before even arriving. I had some fear of heights from experiences in my earlier childhood. I had a tremendous feeling of angst for days and nights. I didn't sleep well (not at all some nights) in anticipation of climbing that god-awful pole.

We were assigned to pole teams on day one of the event, but no indication when, during the program, our team would be called. Every day, during one of the breaks, they would announce and post on the big screens which teams were called to head to the pole-climb area. It was fascinating to me to watch the reactions of people. Many, even most, seemed to clap and cheer, excited and running to the area. That wasn't my reaction!

Finally, on day eight, it finally came; our team number was called, and it was time to go. I was faced with absolute fear. Here I was known as a strong, confident leader, who had taken, by most evaluations, substantial risk in business. Adding to my physical fear, or maybe driving the actual fear response, was the reality that I was showing my vulnerability, and the embarrassment I felt exacerbated what I thought was truly physical fear.

Well of course, I had real references from my childhood about falling off scaffolds, and other height-related issues that could have resulted in serious injury or even death. Of course, that's what was going on here, right? Wow, the strong man was feeling and showing some of who he really was. Less than perfect and worried about how I would be perceived or judged now. I, too, had fears, wanting to be loved and accepted no matter what. Where might that show up in your life?

I was determined (a strong trait) that morning not to climb the pole. Why did I have to? The program doesn't make you climb it. It wasn't a big deal to skip it. I knew it was physically safe but why should I put myself through that level of discomfort? Why?

One of the other coaches, a big well-built Australian guy, approached me and asked what was going on. In coach speak, that's a question that suggests we know there is an issue. I simply told him, I was all set, but this wasn't for me, not important and I didn't need to do it.

As I looked around during the conversation, I noticed so many people, many who would find this climb a daunting physical challenge. The exercise was a personal stretch for people and the approach was for participants to climb to whatever level they could.

This coach engaged me in what I soon would learn and use myself, a great skill and technique to break through the shell and get to the real issues. These vary with all of us and at different times. Our perceptions change and can drive behaviors.

After some deep discussion and coaching, I realized it was in fact important and I would just climb the damn thing rather than live with the wonderment of having stepped back, rationalizing away the real undercurrents driving that fear, and possibly live with regret. Where else has that or will that show up in my life, or yours? *How we play games is often how we play life.*

I can remember the taste of fear in my mouth, the saliva disappearing as I began to place my large wide feet on those little rungs and began ascending. There was a person who held belay for when you jumped from the top to either the trapeze, or freedom. I maintained a mantra as I attempted to remain centered. The more unsettled you were, your energy would affect the pole, and by design it would move around in the mounting and literally oscillate. Talk about adding to the uneasiness.

It is how life works, though. I can recall my legs shaking as I neared the top, still talking aloud to myself, repeating the mantra, I can do this, I can do this! Those little rungs were even smaller now along with the diameter of the pole and I was sure I would pass out. I kept breathing and hearing the cheers of my team below. Their support was monumental.

Well, I made it to the top and the tricky physical part was to now steady myself and attempt to get my size 13's on top of the pole. Gone were the handholds and rungs, it was time to steady oneself to minimize the movement of the pole. I can remember seeing over the palm trees and looking at the beautiful Pacific Ocean for a second before finally jumping into the bliss. It was beyond exhilarating, and liberating on so many levels.

There were so many lessons I documented in my journal from that experience that have truly served me for the past twenty years. As I started to climb, I realized that I had been conditioned for all my life to suppress my fears. I realized that was wrong.

Instead, allow yourself to feel the fear, to engage with it, to challenge its power, to accept it is there, to recognize it is okay to do so, to give yourself permission to be afraid.

At the same time there is a balance. It is important to acknowledge it but not allow it to consume you. You need to know and trust you are bigger, stronger, and guided.

As I climbed I realized so many things about my life. Why allow the thought and feelings of embarrassment about what others think affect you? Why would you and we be here if we were not meant to be? How often do we tell ourselves, no I really don't need to do that. How many times have I said I should and not realized then I must!

I was certainly aware that my physical safety was now entrusted to the person managing the belay system. A person whom I had never met before yet had to decide to place my trust on this day at this moment. What does that say about the speed of trust? How does that compare to the speed with which we trust God and He trusts us?

How then does Kona trust me and I him? To trust that he knows I love him and will always take care of him. For me to know that no matter what is happening in my day, my life, my travel, to never doubt he will love me to death when I arrive home. To know that God loves me and trusts me to love always.

Interestingly that "pole" system designed to wobble as you climb reacts based on your input; it mimics your instability. The less centered and grounded you are, your energy input is met with an equal and opposite reaction. Reflecting, here is another mirror showing up.

As I took the last step, I felt both helpless and free at the same time. In that moment, although there was not anything to hold on to, feeling exposed, the psychology of the exercise included a final distraction, a trapeze twelve feet away.

Despite its distance and the formidable challenge to jump and grab it, it represented the last option for security, something to hold on to rather than what then, simply jumping off? Or falling off? What then do we do in life? Try and avoid the unknown, the bliss that comes with stepping into the unknown, grabbing for that appearance of a lifeline? What if I jump and miss it? I will fall anyway but at least I tried?

Many treated this as a physical challenge and goal to try and jump out and reach the trapeze. If you did catch it, the system would lower you down slowly and gently. The real test and opportunity in the exercise was to not allow that last distraction, the trapeze, the sense of doubt and fear to be self-limiting and as Deepak Chopra would say, just jump off the pole and into the blissful world of the unknown.

To know that we have purpose and to trust our internal guidance system, the Holy Spirit, Jesus, God, Source, Divinity, Mohammed, Buddha, whatever perspective you have on the Supremacy of the Universe to know that we are all guided and responsible to live up to our purpose.

For me in that moment, I was simply trying to breathe, not hyperventilate and pass out, I got my left foot on top, barely touched my right foot and then jumped off! What an amazing feeling as the guy holding belay stopped the fall and lowered me safely. A truly exhilarating breakthrough. I share this example of how fear can compel us to shut down and limit ourselves.

Don't hold fear at arm's-length, to try and suppress it as we have been conditioned; rather, embrace it and let it come to you, ride it rather than letting it ride you, and then move through it.

Limiting ourselves can be interpreted in physical terms. It's not necessarily about having more success, money, fame, it is about being more for you, for God, whatever that means.

It is about being the authentic you. To allow you to see you, and others to see you, rather than conforming to a lower self-standard. It is important to recognize and appreciate that you and I deserve greater abundance in whatever form is right for us.

Fear for fear's sake is not a worthy value. Look at your own story, your own life and find those moments in time when you stepped back, held back, fought against your inner Desire. It's never too late to find you, to love and appreciate you.

It is not for others to decide if you are too old, too young, too fat, too thin, the "wrong" color, you don't have enough money, you don't have the education, or whatever. It is only between you and your Creator and to have the courage to continue developing that trusting relationship.

CHAPTER 21

Twinkle Twinkle Litte Star

(JOE)

I remember a wonderful night on an overnight camping trip with the Scouts. It was part of my journey to the next level and it included me needing to get a merit badge for "Stars." Fred woke me up at 3 a.m. and we walked through the crisp air to an open field. I recall the mountains, the early morning dew on my feet. I could feel damp air down low but crisper air above. I remember to this day, staring up at the abundance of the night sky. The millions of sparkling lights, those stars, the planets, and constellations.

Before Fred asked me the formal test questions, he suggested I just look and ponder for a few minutes. Here I was, an inner-city kid in the middle of this field being given an extraordinary gift by a wonderful man. A man I know was sent to me by God to help shape my journey. It was all part of my story, really. How is that some thirty-five-plus years later I realized what a profound impact this one man had on my life.

I was sitting with a close friend, Bob, at my get-away vacation place in New Hampshire, on the deck talking about how much I, and we, loved hiking, climbing mountains, and the outdoors. I was so proud of my skills in the wilderness. So proud of being in touch and connected to nature but forgetting, or not remembering, maybe not reflective enough due to the blistering pace of life, how Fred was the catalyst so many years before.

Suffice it to say, in life, no matter where we are, we need a slow-down, a time to look not only deep inside, but also back. This helps us recall where we came from, what's behind --, and never look back as primary view, but as a driver.

Our focus must be on the road ahead, all the while being present in the moment and grateful for where we are right now. We can't get to where we want and deserve to be from a place of resistance. We must know we are, in fact, right where we are supposed to be, to where we designed and attracted ourselves to be. A room doesn't go from darkness to light without a switch. Accepting where we are is the switch. We grow from where we are planted.

● ● ● ●

One of the toughest and scary moments I experienced was the decision to leave my first high-level senior executive corporate job. I was realizing the value system I ascribe to was no longer in play. It was late 2013 and it was time to move on and do some different things, new experiences, while not indicting the past ones, as they had served me well for the time. The environment had become toxic and was not in alignment with my desires.

I always prided myself on remembering where I came from, not being pretentious, having not been raised with a silver spoon in my mouth. It is interesting to have been in the corporate environment around all types of leaders, blessed to have some of the best -- and the worst.

It is remarkable even with a strong constitution, how when subjected to constant negative reinforcement, self-doubt creeps in, grows to affect your behavior in and outside the work place. It begins to chip away at your identity.

I worked for an individual who had ulterior motives, not of becoming of a leader, but being self-serving and destructive. We had our own version of the Star Wars character, the "dark lord." I felt not only myself changing but also some of the most respected executives I knew. Trust was broken. It felt like being emotionally suffocated while bearing the significant pressure to perform, the responsibilities of the aircraft we were building, and the lives of thousands of our employees and their families.

These moments can be very difficult; the feelings of uncertainty, the underlying drive to make a change. Was it about choice or fear of the existing? Was it really to do something different, who knew for sure at the time. The "Why" becomes most relevant. A combination of circumstances can exacerbate a situation, leaving you perplexed about what you are doing.

My mother was elderly now and her health was failing. She was such a powerful and independent woman, never needy, and we were not conditioned to assisting. Our son had returned from several combat tours in Iraq, so it felt like it was time to move back to the East Coast, back to Connecticut, after a couple of years in the Midwest.

I went to work as a consultant for a very small business owned by people I knew, loved, and respected. I was envisioning being close to my family and living at least part time in the mountains of New Hampshire, but I was not ready for the change.

Kona would be there for me the entire time. We would continue going on hikes and climbs, as he gained more and more endurance. He helped me stay grounded and to manage my feelings of worry (not an emotion I experienced often, until then), rather to know it was all part of the process.

● ● ● ●

(KONA)

It was arguably a four- to six-month period of the greatest darkness Joe experienced in his life. How was it possible, to have come so far, the inner-city kid, accomplished now, leading large organizations in aerospace, who raised a family, traveled and lived in many areas, had a beautiful home -- yet he felt so lost and afraid?

He didn't know how to worry, but the Jack in me is a worrier and I knew he was in fact troubled. I was sure it was time for him to make a move, and in the end, it was a step along the journey of a yet to be, bolder and deeper change. It is through these experiences of resistance that show up in a variety of ways, including dark moments, fear, doubt, emotional pain, lashing out at those we love, yet being led to recognize that this can happen and is part of the progression.

CHAPTER 22

Inner Demons

(KONA)

It was becoming clear to me that the Mountain Man was dealing with some heavier demons now. This impacted his ability to allow himself the gifts of liberation and freedom to become more in alignment with what he wanted.

There was a period where it seemed like I was the only creature, place, or thing in his life that remained true and consistent with him, behaviorally. Isn't that strange one should or might ask. How can that be, sure or not, I am a dog!

He has a loving family, wife, kids, friends. He still certainly loved and cared for them but clearly his patterns and attitude of typically being strong, positive, and reinforcing were not showing up with them. His focus, anger, and frustrations were, though!

I was watching, studying and observing. I remained true to him and for the first time, I worried about my pack leader. You know, us "Jacks" do worry. We carry emotional pain and pull it away from our human companions. So, how was it I ever considered, that he would love me, still play with me (a bit less to be true), but otherwise no change. Enzo saw and experienced the same behavioral changes as the family did. Joe would at times be unkind to Enzo. This surprised me as he had adopted Enzo from a rescue place out in St. Louis.

What was it about me that was so different? I knew, but maybe he was learning what this was all about. If I was his "spiritual mirror" and he was upset with himself, I never experienced any of it. Was it rather that he knew or felt I expressed true unconditional love for him? Never judged him, never treated him any other way no matter what?

Humans, like dogs, can and do have health conditions that can affect their behavior. He went to a human doctor, I guess, similar to our canine docs to assess if he was okay physically. They apparently found a few issues that needed some adjustment and it helped him to start showing back up as Mountain Man! Ahhh yes, time for all of us to go again!

The anguish, sleepless nights and confusion he experienced back then was a vital part of his journey.

I knew it, he may not have, and I share this story to help one see and use it as a mirror in your own life. All of you face trials and tribulations. These are simple techniques to get you back to why you are really here, and to take full advantage of the time you have gracefully been given.

Gratitude is so powerful. Joe gets get a constant reminder of that power daily with me. I, like many dogs, am always so happy to see him and thankful. Humans often feel there is an innocence in dogs being grateful. You know they believe it is simply that dogs are in the moment, have short memory and live as if we haven't seen our humans since forever. It is more than that really, as it should be for humans. Every day you have an opportunity to start with gratitude or squander the time. How many things can you tell yourself you are grateful for?

● ● ● ●

(JOE)

Here is a simple daily exercise. Whatever calendar day it is, write down the number of things you are grateful for. For example, if it is the thirty-seventh day of the year, you need to find thirty-seven things for which to be grateful. It builds momentum as you get deeper in the calendar. You can stretch this to be yearly and build up for all 365 days. This or similar exercises can shift your attention and focus dramatically and put you in place where you feel really good, peaceful and receptive.

It is full circle, we then love us more, love God more, attract more and are in the closed loop of manifesting greater, more empowering experiences to enrich our lives and the lives of those we love the most.

Sometimes we allow our desire and focus to serve as blinders to our peripheral vision and miss important clues. Sometimes there are clues for our loved ones in our family, our work, our social circles. At times we miss these vital signals for ensuring we are looking after ourselves. Our desires, our needs, our wants and well-being.

Kona continues to show me more about myself. He helps in allowing me to see my blind spots that I hadn't seen before. To experience time seeming to stop, to let go of one's personal "stuff," to understand and experience, even if for a moment, true unconditional love, unbounded, unabated, unforced, beyond the ego and conscious mind, for someone outside of ourselves. And yes, to experience that same relentless, never-ending, beautiful and celestial self-love.

To the casual observer, these would seemingly be "cute" and or a "cool" thing between a man and his dog. But look down, dive down deeper in that pond, see what is below the surface. It may appear dark and muddy, but it is there where we find our soul, rich with nutrients, coded with Desire, embedded with a spiritual guidance system to help us navigate to our highest and best. One needs only to learn and master the courage to peek, and much will be found.

● ● ● ●

(KONA)

Mountain Man Joe would face some ongoing challenges and yet he would lean on me and push through all the adversity and fear. Enzo and I knew to stay close to him. I made sure we had our play time in the morning. Wow he loves to play this game he calls "KA-KA." I basically roll on my back and we end up in a wrestling match. He has me conditioned that when he takes his hands and makes a squeezing motion with his fingers, I know it is time! I then would do the drop and roll and let out a "ka-ka, ka-ka" yelp. I truly love the game; I get a great belly rub and afterward he massages my shoulders.

More than anything though, it is dedicated focused time and all about love. Yes, this little twenty-three pound, hot-shot canine has the Pack Leader under control.

By this summer, I was already six and soon to be seven years old in the fall. We have enjoyed much together and climbed mountains, taken long walks and what my humans call hikes, taken rides in the car, gone out to "doggie dinners" together and played with lots of other canines. We have been given the best food, they take us to this great, what is called a "Pet Salon" where we get a bath, our fur brushed and trimmed, our nails clipped. Wow, these humans spoil us with love, why do they need to do that?

CHAPTER 23

Transformation

(JOE)

So many people think this is a typical story about a man and his dog. And for some, perhaps that's what they are receiving. To me, though, this love story is about a man who overcame much, who transformed from being afraid to look in the mirror to wonder about what he would really see, to know that he is blessed to have attracted an amazing creature, who in so many ways, came in a form that has similar characteristics and personality.

The dog (spelt backward is god, small "g"), taught me so many crucial lessons about just being in the moment. Kona opened my eyes to what really matters in life and what doesn't. He has been there for me through some of the most difficult and confusing times in my life; always providing that steady smiling happy I love you no matter what and will you please go love you too!

I learned my mission was to be there for him. To realize he is a bridge, that God, our Creator, wants and needs my, and our, love. That He too was lonely and in need of sharing and connection. To never forget about the abundance available. To climb higher, let the wind blow through your hair, feel the sun in your face, the sand on your feet, to fear not, to Trust Divinity, to know that we are here to live purpose, to love and be loved, to know we matter, to always know we are guided.

That we are in the end Spirits enjoying a human experience. To know we all need a "mirror" to help us see our true faces. To stop hiding and get rid of the dirty secrets, to live authentically and with integrity. To be able to pull off the cover and masks and no matter what, see and share the real you -- and love it, by enjoying the moment. One thing is for sure, we don't know how much physical time we have here in this phase but how we spend it is up to us.

I look forward to growing older with Kona, and while today I cannot imagine a life without him, I simply must know and trust all will be as it should be. There are so many more mountains to climb, places to go, experiences to enjoy.

How does lack of self-love really show up? What does it look and feel like? Many don't know this is at the root of their behaviors. It can show up in many forms. Anger, frustration, and what appears at the surface to be typical reactions to life events, are only masks to the underlying cause.

It's not about what is in our DNA, it is the conditioned expectation for a "man." We are supposed to be strong, the ones who should not show real emotions. All these are not novel concepts, in their own right. But they may be inextricably linked to the lack of self love.

CHAPTER 24

Unbounded Love

(KONA)

It was a Friday night, and I remember Mountain Man was relaxing watching a game my human companions called hockey. These two-legged creatures wear some strange-looking shiny sharp things on their feet and slide around on a cold slippery surface known as ice. We canines have paws and claws to help with traction. I would think if humans were meant to run around on the ice, they would have the same.

These contraptions on their feet are not big like snowshoes, they are designed to let them glide while carrying wooden sticks and slapping this hard, black item around they call a puck. Strange . . . .

Later that night, it was time for Enzo and me to go out for our final potty before snuggling and bed time. Wow I do love to sneak in under the covers with Mr. D. I feel so secure with him and I know he does with me. So, Mom D let us out. You know by now, we live in this great house on the lake and lots of critters for us to chase -- and some for us to be chased.

We love the place so much. Lots of woods and trees, places to dig, oh the smells especially in the Spring time! And those chipmunks and squirrels. The terrier in me is hard-wired to chase them. Yes, I have doggie A.D.D.! Squirrel! Where, where??

These creatures have their way with us most of the time. They climb trees fast and then chatter to taunt us. Lately Enzo and I have found a way to trick and trap them. We really want to play but often they end up dying from the rough-housing.

Close to the house, there is what humans call a forest. Looks like trees to me but when they are grouped up in huge bunches they give it a name. It is an amazing playground with places to run, hide, and dig – but also filled with variety of predators of all shapes and sizes. Some pose a real threat to me and larger ones even to big broad and strong Enzo.

One specie is called coyotes and they are in the forest. They seem similar to dogs, much larger than me, but are closer to our wolf descendants. They are pack animals and rarely travel alone. They are nasty critters and almost seem to enjoy brutalizing their victims in an attack.

They love to feed on deer and will attack from the rear, damaging the hind quarters, their butts, and let them slowly die by bleeding to death, while they chase yet another. They hunt together and don't often play alone. There are also bears (that would not be a fair fight), bobcats, raccoons, fox, eagles, owls, and snakes. Most of these excite me.

The Jack Russell in me is a fighter, I stand up to anyone. It is like Joe D, pack leader, the Bronx kid who now has more confidence and courage and rarely will back down from a confrontation, yet another reason I was sent in my form. Like a "southy" Irishman from Boston, this little twenty-three pounder won't allow himself to be pushed around and certainly not allow anyone to mess with Enzo or my human pack!

We love to roam, and since sometimes we don't necessarily return home when called, Enzo and I are forced to wear these special collars around our necks. Mom did this to protect us. It works by emitting an electrical "zap" if we cross the boundary of the property. As we approach the boundary it emits a beeping sound to warn us of the impending shock. It doesn't really hurt but is uncomfortable. Humans know the Pavloff story so really Enzo and I are conditioned now that we don't really need the collars. We get near the boundary and we immediately start to hesitate and brace.

It is interesting when pack leader takes us for a walk outside the property. I'm smart so I know my *collar is off. Enzo still hesitates as he is expecting the dreadful shock.*

That night when we went out to do our business before bed, I did my pee, and so did Enzo. We then heard a noise down at the end of the driveway. It is one of our primary jobs to investigate anything and everything that might enter our yard, human or not, and alert the pack leaders.

As I honed my vision on the outskirt of the property and turned my sniffer in the direction of the sounds, I saw a creature, much larger than our squirrel or chipmunk friends walking just into our yard and across the grass area. I said, "Enzo, I'll go check it out! You go around the other side." I started to run and turned on my warning bark. It is kind of a high-pitched, not whimsical, hey pal look out, here I come, you better leave our territory. We are very territorial you know.

I just hate it when I come back from being away and walk the yard and smell all the violators who have penetrated the territory while we were away. As I came around my favorite oak tree, I came face-to-face with a big fat raccoon. Yes, it was a raccoon and looked like this boy had plenty to eat. I would guess he was all of twenty-eight or thirty pounds. He looked healthy.

We stared at each other for what seemed like minutes, I kicked my bark into the "I feel threatened" mode, and he refused to back away. My hackles were now up as was my heart rate. This could get ugly and fast. Where the heck was Enzo? Then I saw him coming around from the backside. I was emboldened now with backup.

These racoons have very articulate and sharp claws. They go for the eyes. The pug in me means I have large eyes, not quite the obnoxious ones on a full pug, but certainly they would be a target for this big boy.

As Enzo approached I increased the pitch and tempo of my bark and took one step toward the rac-coon, intending to make him back away. There was no chance I would step back. Before I knew it we were in a full-fledged Irish brawl!

He was strong and snarly, biting at me and using those razor-sharp claws to scrape at me and my eyes. I was using my terrier teeth to grab and tear at him. I also used my svelte, some say thick and powerful hind legs to make a wrestling move on him. You know, use his portliness against him. This was painful for both of us and the screaming was loud and intense.

Enzo soon grabbed him from the back and was trying to pull him off me. I felt his teeth puncture my forehead above my eyes while he was clawing at my eyes. The screams became more intense and he surely was feeling the result of Enzo using those jaws to yank at him. I know I was doing some damage to him with my teeth. He had a firm grasp on me while he continued biting and scraping.

In the meantime, Mom D heard the screaming and immediately ran into the house to get pack leader. He was falling asleep watching the hockey game, but *she startled him from his rest. She told him something was wrong, very wrong! By the time he came outside the screaming was even more elevated. There were screams of pain for sure, he knew. He had been very concerned about the coyotes in the area as they could be heard most nights howling as they ran nearby.*

In his still half-asleep condition, he was convinced the coyotes had grabbed and were tearing his precious Spirit friend Kona apart! He heard my screams. He took off running shoeless with reckless abandon toward the sounds into the darkness of night all the while yelling my name at the top of his lungs. "Kona, Kona, Kona, where are you??!!!"

As he approached the sounds near the big tree, dark and adjacent to it was an evergreen (another great place to dig) with lots of low branches and brush. There was clearly commotion in the area and without lights he couldn't make out what was happening. He remained convinced coyotes had me. He had no idea where Enzo was and it was hard to make out any-thing in the darkness.

In the frenzy, and with his full-on adrenaline, he became aware of this thrashing around under the tree. Enzo was still trying to detach the fatty raccoon off me and as we, this massive ball of fur, came out from under the tree, Mountain Man was now sure the large dark object hinged to me was in fact a coyote.

His heart was racing, he was still yelling my name out loud. It was the fog of war in that moment. How many coyotes, he wondered? Would Mom D come out with guns in time? Would he be able to save Kona? Where the hell was Enzo? It was such a blur. In the blackness of night, mistakenly thinking Enzo was a coyote, he then, with all his might, squarely kicked him in his side. Enzo tried to say, "Kona tell him it's me!"

What happened next was remarkable! He reached down in the darkness blindly and ended up literally picking up this brawling ball of **dog and raccoon**. He was desperately trying to pull us apart but we were in our own fighting frenzy and locked on to each other.

In the murkiness of the melee, my spirit partner was enduring wounds, too, deep scratches and bites. It seemed not to phase him at all. He continued and finally broke the lock and launched the beast, while trying to secure me in his arms. He was exhausted and out of breath from the fear, yelling, and adrenaline.

The raccoon lunged and ran right back at us and Joe swiftly and firmly kicked him away. I was out of control, my own adrenaline pumping. I was truly all "jacked up," as humans would say. Mom D was out there now too and in her own emotional state. Joe realized then what had happened, saw Enzo and knew he was trying to help.

Pack leader ran me into the house and tried to calm both of us down. At the same time, I knew the raccoon was injured and Joe was preparing to put the wounded animal down. Enzo had a different idea and finished the business.

He used his powerful jaws and neck to grab the critter and violently shake the life out of it. Mom reported *that Enzo finished the job. My leader then tended to my wounds, lovingly petted me and loved me.*

He would often tell people he would do anything for me. That night, he showed me that was ever so true! How was it that this man, without regard for himself, unknowing of the actual danger, would do that for me, a dog? It didn't matter if it was a raccoon, coyote, bear, eagle, or any threat, I know he wouldn't have acted any different. Yes, I am technically a dog, but this is so much more than a man's reaction to or for a dog. I am sure by this point you get that!

This was so much more -- and deeper. This was him really fulfilling his mission. It was to love me, to learn more about the simple side of love and caring, that boundaries and limitations only stand in the way of our ability to see us for who we are – this was my proof that yes, we are both on a mission. A mission perhaps that could be described as necessary to save each other.

A mission of spiritual connection, a story of unbounded love for other beings no matter their form. A different kind of love story between three spirits: the Creator, a man and a dog.

It is how God loves us no matter what. He is there for us even when we can't see it or feel it. He chooses and desires us to partner with Him in helping with Creation. He will do anything for us, to save us, and to love us -- and He craves the same.

I am so much more than a dog, you know. I am a lesson in the humility and courage to put aside

141

judgment, criticism, and obstacles. I know now, that while I worked hard and diligently for nearly ten years to be the mirror in his life, to show God in many funny and serious ways, he has learned much and changed much.

His love for self has grown more and I know he has faced the fear of his own mortality and that of mine. I am proud to be his spiritual partner. I, too, have grown, also understanding how humans face their own demons with the blessing of free will.

I am ten years old now, and while I am fed healthy food and get lots of exercise, even for a "jack breed," humans would say that in dog years I am getting to be an old man. I still feel spry, strong, and love to go on walks and hikes with him. I may have lost a step, but as long as I'm able I will continue to be by his side.

CHAPTER 25

Tested

(JOE)

It was a challenging 2016, as I was still feeling the need to do something different. I had a fabulous opportunity to work and live in Switzerland for two years. It was near Geneva, in a town called Morges, on lake Geneva, the mostly French-speaking part of the country.

My mom had passed away the year before, I finished a two-year stint as COO of a public aerospace company where a combination of circumstances in a heavily political and lack of accountability work place meant it was time to move on. Our daughter was diagnosed with a serious health issue, a rare cancer, and our son, who returned from heavy combat tours in Iraq, was battling the demons of PTSD.

Given these challenges, we delayed plans to move to Switzerland and focused on all we could do to help our daughter fight the terrible disease. Family always comes first for me, so I found a good interim position back in Connecticut and we moved back East.

It is all about perception in life and choices we make for the things we can control. At this time, nothing mattered more than Jenna's health and we would do anything to support her.

During times of great difficulty, we are given an opportunity to grow stronger. It is also an opportunity to see ourselves as victims. One might ask, why and how me? Or ponder if we are in fact energetic spiritual beings having a human experience?

How then is it that we would attract such unwanted experiences in our lives? How would anyone attract cancer intentionally? How then, does this all really work? Is it only a convenient belief that when things go our way and manifestations of what we call "good" or "great" show up, the magnet is on? How can that be?

Laws of the Universe are either in play or not. The Universe isn't emotional, is it? Gravity doesn't decide to show up today and not tomorrow. It doesn't care if it rains or the sun shines, if we are crying or smiling, laughing and feeling joy, or sad and sorrowful. No, it is consistent and uniform.

So then how would it be that energy laws, magnetic laws, would have such seemingly built-in incongruency? When and how does that work? The powerful laws of attraction don't give us the power to attract something in someone else's life.

Suffice it to say, we need to be careful and pay close attention to what we focus on. Like does attract like. It is easy to think we are targeting what we want when in fact we are precisely centered on the lack of what we desire. Yes, we can be laser-pointed to exactly what we don't want in our lives -- and then get more of it! When we focus on the lack of money, health, safety, security, love and worthiness. we end up with more "lack."

This is not a story or book on the deep prescriptive approaches to those laws, but rather a simpler guideline as to how they work. Be very mindful and attentive to how you feel, as well as how you "think" about what you want. It is not practical to manage the thousands upon thousands of thoughts we have in a day. Make it easy, define some rules to feel good.

Kona has allowed me to feel good or even great at times when my situation has been, shall we say, much less than optimal. All I need to do is see him, have him run up to me, jump in my arms, do the dog-lick-my-face thing, stroke his fur and my state changes. It sounds so simple and it is, yet not always easy.

It is all about realizing we are moving up an emotional scale. It is actually how we vibrate, our magnetic frequency; the better the mood or emotional state, the higher our vibrational response to the Universe.

Find what helps you get closer and closer to a higher vibration, resulting in part, from how you feel. This creates a stronger magnetic field, bringing into your life those people, places and things necessary to experience what you really want and are in alignment with your true Desire.

Let's be clear, I'm a first-generation Italian-American kid from the inner city of New York. I had parents who cared about me and my brother and sister, but we certainly were on the lower socio-economic scale. I wasn't privileged or was able to afford attending prominent universities. My mom and dad made big sacrifices to send me to Catholic grammar and high school.

At that time in the Bronx, it was a better way to have some influence on the environment with common values. I did very well in grammar school, which opened up the opportunity to attend Cardinal Spellman.

I did well there, but could have done even better. I spent too much time enjoying myself, hanging with some kids who were smart, good souls, but partied too much and weren't as focused as they/we should've been on academics.

After my famous "rock star" night at that concert, in the wee hours of that morning when I prayed and promised God, get me out of this and I will move to achieve my highest and my best, it did change everything!

I blasted out of the Bronx and into the exciting world of aerospace where I have worked on some of the most sophisticated and advanced military aircraft for generations to come. I started my college career at the Academy of Aeronautics and studied aeronautical engineering. I have loved airplanes since I was a little boy and have never grown tired of watching them fly. Even a deep knowledge of how they work never ceases to amaze me as to what they can do and how they do it.

Interestingly, but not surprisingly as I look back to that time at the beginning of college, I worked in the deli of my friend Albo's dad. As you might expect, it was called Tony's deli on a corner in the Bronx. It was more than a place for people to shop, it was a sort of communal gathering typical in Italian neighborhoods where people would hang out and just talk to each other.

I can remember telling Albo that someday I would be working in really cool and advanced aerospace programs. I can recall visualizing seeing myself going to work where I needed special badges to enter special access classified areas. I consciously knew nothing about the law of attraction back then, even though it was in play. It is always in play for you and me, by the way. Those visuals and the associated feelings I had absolutely and precisely showed up in my life.

Check in where you had past visualizations combined with emotion and they showed up in your life. Times when your attraction magnet was on full power!

I have held senior executive positions in several private and public companies, consulted and owned and operated businesses. I don't share this to be boastful about my personal accomplishments, surely to be considered modest by some and extraordinary by others. It is really to share the art of the possible, how things work, really work. It is not about a mechanical process, of A+B+C.

These are resultant manifestations and actions that come through our spiritual connection to our deeper desire and our magnetic ability to attract what we want and need in our lives.

For example, Kona's mission is philosophically simple and clear. It is partly to keep me at a higher vibrational level, to teach me and remind me how to feel good even though circumstances suggest otherwise.

It has also helped me to be in the "moment;" to simply sit on the deck at the house and look at the moonlight glistening on the lake, the quietness, the darkness of the wooded areas and to just be ever present in that moment, without a past or future, just be there through and through!

That brings a level of deep connection in and of itself with the inner me, closer to the Almighty, closer to mission, purpose, love, and worthiness without judgment or condition.

To have Kona sit next to me and know no worries about yesterday or tomorrow, just totally focused on that moment and experience gratitude for all in my life. Kona taught and helped me learn to compartmentalize my life. To be 100% present in what I am doing in the moment, whether it is practicing the piano for thirty minutes, praying, working, exercising, teaching, playing, laughing, or crying. Just be there with all your heart, mind and spirit!

CHAPTER 26

The Transfer

(JOE)

In early 2017, despite months of great progress, Jenna's cancer decided to re-engineer itself and the tumor in her adrenal gland grew rapidly and spawned a new one in a precarious area. How could this be, why now? Were my priorities not right? Was this about me? Was I once again not good enough and being punished through my children?

Even after all the work I have done to feel the power of me and the love of me, Kona lessons, loving him so I could love me and love God and love the world and life, even more? The growth I have had in my life, the study of the law of attraction, the stuff that

I coach and teach, the authenticity and congruency I hold so dear ... why then? She clearly didn't deserve it.

We had been through so much, always looking at things through the positive lens, -- and knowing that things happen for a reason: "the "pinball machine," that night in February at the concert, the begging for my life back, the coaching I've done, the hard work to provide for my family selflessly.

Really ... my father wasn't enough, all my mom did, all the gratitude I thought I had and showed, our son in combat and almost losing him, the constantly trying to see the good ... it all came crashing down on me on a night in January, 2017.

I was in a hotel room on a business trip when Jenna called me to tell me the news, the bad news. The cancer had a major resurgence with a vengeance, and the new tumor, outside the adrenal gland, was metastasizing.

I thought a shower would help, as end-of-the-day showers were my way of cleansing before rest, getting rid of the dirt of the day. As I felt the clean hot water on my body, all the emotion came raging out, directed at God, Jesus, my friend and Spirit. I was, and felt, alone. Kona wasn't there to help and it wouldn't have mattered that night.

I never before in my life lashed out at Him so viciously, without an iota of reverence, in the most direct and Bronx-like terms. I remember pounding on the walls of that shower stall with all my might. It wasn't a blaming, but rather a transfer of ultimate responsibility. "You say you walk with Me and YOU will carry my burdens, when I see the one set of foot-prints in the sand and felt abandoned, it was then that

YOU carried me, well here you go BIG GUY, you got it all, I am done and I can't do this anymore".

You say ask and receive and I have done that before, but not like this. It is all on you now. I am taking you at your Word like never before. This dialogue went on for probably thirty or more minutes. I was almost in a trance. When I was done I was exhausted and fell asleep.

Over the next few days, God graced me with a peace about the event. I didn't feel guilty. I received a message that I spoke to Him as directly without confusion in my own terms, albeit Bronx vernacular. I did ask with precision and clarity, I did surrender, I did call for Him to come.

While I was confident that my priorities of family and in this case, Jenna, were right, there were a few distractions still hanging. I was still holding on to the possibility of going to Switzerland.

After that night, I let it all go and focused entirely on being present for my daughter and anything and everything I could do as a loving dad to help, realizing the responsibility was not mine to solve.

It is those moments of pain and darkness that we have the glorious opportunity to let go of our fears, our perception of control, ask God, The Universal Truth, with clarity, and then transfer the burden and responsibility. Stand back and let it work as it should. Know the answer will come in a form that is as it must be.

Through prayer, medicine, natural-healing techniques and protocols, Jenna fought the cancer with incredible determination. She never allowed herself to surrender to its power, but rather constantly believed in her ability to draw on God to help her focus on and attract into her life the things she needed to win the fight. It is when we ask with precision, that we get the answers, although not always in the form we envision.

If life is worth living it is worth recording. Many people journal and I learned the value of taking the time to reflect on my day and memorialize the magical moments along with the challenges. I would free flow and simply write for a few minutes each night before going to sleep. I haven't always been regimented to the daily routine, but on balance have been "journaling" for over twenty years. I have taught this exercise, and the connection to gratitude it provides, to others including my children.

About a month after that memorable night in the shower, Jenna called me to tell me she had a vivid vision during the night. I asked her what it was and she said she could not share with me or anyone. She said it was bright, clear, and rocked her to the core.

We have always had a close and deep relationship so I found her partial sharing confusing. She was shaken by the experience so the best advice I could muster was to remind her of the value of chronicling life through daily writing. I had no idea where this would lead. Nor did she.

The next few months were a roller coaster ride of emotions, ranging from hope to worry, fear, anger, frustration, love, hate, confidence, faith you name it. "Ride the ride," I reminded myself. Sure it is philosophically simple but definitely not easy.

● ● ● ●

(KONA)

During that time, I would do my best to physically be close to the Mountain Man, my human. As I would snuggle up on his lap, my breathing would match his. My larger than life puppy dog eyes would lock on to his. I could feel what he felt, I sensed his pain and I would experience the anxiety in my body. I would pant at a high frequency, my nose and mouth would be dry, We were inextricably connected.

• • • •

(JOE)

Roughly four months after that hostile night in the shower, and three months since Jenna had the "vision", our family, as customary, were at church for Good Friday service. Jenna seemed distant and pre-occupied, not surprising given her condition. Her life was at stake so her behavior was understandable. We certainly didn't appreciate their was more, much more going on.

After the service, we went back to Jenna's house, and again she seemed aloof, yet capricious. What was going on I began to wonder? She then asked me to please wear something nice as we would be going out to dinner. Mo and I looked at each other oddly as we considered Good Friday a day of reverence, humility, and respect for the incredible sacrifice Jesus made for humanity. We traditionally spent the day at home in a reflective state. We simply did not understand why Jenna would suggest otherwise.

Our curiosity grew as she asked us to please sit down in her living room. Mo and I sat on that couch as Jenna stood before of us with a teacher-like manner. She held a book in her hand and asked if I knew what it was. Certainly I knew, as it was a Bible I gave her many years before.

In an instructional style, she informed us that there were secrets in the Bible. We acknowledged it and were becoming more perplexed as to what was going on here. At one point I told her there were likely dozens, maybe hundreds of secrets in the Book. What was the point?

She handed the book to Mo asking her to find the secret. She obliged and quickly flipped through it and said she had found it! I stared at her with a dazed look of acceptance.

Mo then handed me the Bible to look for and see if I could also find the "secret." I was now beyond confused and bewildered, and moving toward frustration.

Jenna gave a clue by asking if I remembered one of her favorite Scriptures. I struggled to recall it and she provided a further hint, it was related to one of her tattoos! I then vaguely remembered it was likely Isaiah, but not the specific verse! She had inked the words of Isaiah (40:31, "…those who hope in the Lord will renew their strength. They will soar on wings like eagles; they will run and not grow weary, they will walk and not be faint") on the side of her abdomen several years earlier. The same side of her body where the cancer was now thriving.

After several minutes of what seemed to be a strange tutorial, I started flipping through the pages looking for Isaiah. As I came upon it, a few pages into the book of Isaiah, I noticed a small piece of white paper. It was a piece torn from notebook paper to create a sort of bookmark. On it was a hand-written set of words.

The next few moments were dreamlike, as time slowed and virtually stopped. I realized all that had been happening that day, her somewhat bizarre behavior, the clues, were starting to coalesce and make sense. As I started to read the note on that little piece of paper, my brain was jumping around trying to get to the outcome.

It was in fact a note Jenna had written months before. Specifically when she had the vision and we discussed her noting it! The vision she had, translated into words, on this bookmark in the Book of Isaiah said effectively, "It is Good Friday, and I see myself telling my family that I am cancer-free. Please Lord tell me I am not imagining this!"

I read that note and remained stunned and mystified. Surely she must be trying to tell us this was her vision for the following year. Surely she couldn't be telling us that this raging out of control, with a mind of its own, sugar loving, oxygen hating cancer was gone? How could that be? We were all definitely hopeful but there was such a long way to go. The malignancy had been going in the wrong direction. What the hell was going on here?

Jenna relieved us of the puzzle when she briefly left the room, returning with a fine bottle of champagne and proclaimed, "You guys don't get it, I'm cancer-free!!"

Whaaaaattt? How could it be ?She wasn't scheduled to have a PET scan (a special screening that illuminates cancer cells) until the following week, how would she know this?

To add to what we believe is a miracle, her doctor's office had called her earlier in the week with a request to change her upcoming PET scan appointment. Recognizing Good Friday was a holiday for many people, they asked Jenna if she would come in for the scan that morning? Yes, Good Friday morning.

Jenna had been carrying that vision with her for months and I can only imagine what ran through her mind when she got that phone call. It was all lining up; yes, the answer was coming.

The behavior earlier in the day at church made sense now. She had the test results several hours earlier, the doctors were amazed to the point of repeating the test and ordering additional screens for validation.

Yes, we broke tradition and went out to dinner that night with the greatest level of gratitude and excitement. We made phone calls to friends and family to share the incredible news.

As I took some time to reflect. I had flashbacks of that night in the shower. The ultimate "ask and you shall receive." Thoughts of that cold February concert night so many years before, where I made Him a promise.

There is no doubt Jenna was in alignment with her desire. I was, and remain in awe, of the ability we have to connect with a Supreme God. The sense of responsibility I feel now to continue evolving, growing, teaching and giving back. Jenna's cancer story was a must on so many levels. The amalgamation of the puzzle pieces, the bumpers in the "pinball" machine, the real ask with clarity and the trust created an earthquake running through my body, vibrating me to the core.

After Jenna's subsequent tests over the next six months confirmed she was still cancer-free, situation stabilized, I realized I could get back to my own story and focus on me and what I desired. I realized I still needed to make some changes and get on with what I was passionate about in life. For me, something about health, wellness, and coaching had to be part of the plan.

We currently own an amazing business that provides an extraordinary program that combines the very best fitness classes, nutritional counseling, and motivational support to help our members achieve fast and lasting results for their health, appearance and fitness levels, in a fun, no-judgment and loving environment.

The journey I have been on and the help Kona provided to teach me more about love, connection to my Creator and my own real desire came through the vast series of hurdles and experiences that were both fun and exciting and others that were down-right painful.

When you really love you, it opens your peripheral vision to an extent you didn't see before or thought possible. The opportunities are endless; as you feel better and better, your magnetic attraction kicks into high gear and you draw in more people, places, and events that are in alignment with you truest desire. The speed of the manifestations increase exponentially!

CHAPTER 27

The End is the Beginning

(KONA)

Later in 2018, Joe, Mountain Man was sitting on the chair in the kitchen, staring out at the beautiful lake. I had a sense he needed some love. I did my typical walk over, sit at the bottom of the chair with a big, please pick me up look; yeah, I can jump up but prefer for you to reach down and haul me up into your arms.

It worked again. I was soon off the ground, in his sinewy and embracing arms, just loving it when he lets me lick his face and he then calmly and rhythmically pets my coat.

The weather was warming so I was shedding more than usual, and hair and fur were everywhere.

By this point, though, it didn't matter anymore. Good thing he has grown past "hair mattering."

As he stared out that window, I was sure he wanted to make a change and do something else with his life now. This time, yes, for real. He was growing and evolving, thank you very much. He did seem to still love the chase, the adventure of it all. The need and want to be wanted. No matter what, he seemed to deny time elapsing.

He continues to have what appears to be boundless energy and enthusiasm, refusing to consider himself aging, regardless what anyone or data would suggest. How dare you tell him he would not or could not! How dare you tell this Mountain Man, this Italian Bronx kid, who lived and died a thousand times with pain and loss of his father, the suffering of his mom, the jubilation of his mother's love and belief, the connection and grounding of his Spirit friend Kona, that there were limits and boundaries.

I've watched him for nearly a decade now and know him as few others do. And please, stop with the telling me "what a cute dog" and "they all love, etc." **Yes, but what you should know, really know, and understand is our forms are irrelevant.**

Transformations happen, engagement with his true authentic self enhanced. Many experiences, although painful at the time, were designed to help him with navigation.

I love this human and he has given me back so much love, too. He has shown me he is more than capable of limitless and unconditional, boundless love. No doubt we have fostered growth in each other, a deeper understanding and appreciation for what we have in common versus differences. Regardless of how much time we have together here, when we are back with our Creator, the mission will have gone well.

He has allowed me into his life as God's ambassador, to carry the message that God, too, is loved, that He, the Supreme One, need not be or feel lonely or forgotten.

And . . . that the Creation of many species, in varying forms, ensures He could share abundance, and that was, in fact working and complete.

So, this is the story of love. A real but different kind of love story. A distinctive kind of trilogy. Love between a man and his best friend, a spiritual being who came to him in the form of a dog named Kona, that he manifested through the magnificent law and power of attraction.

I am more than a friend, guide, and mirror; I am a conduit, a pipeline for feedback to and from God. Joe is also on a multi-purpose mission. For much, if not all of his life, this man searched for what was missing, what could be bigger, better, how to feel whole, how to ultimately experience the person he so outwardly demonstrates to others.

But how to feel it for himself, in the privacy of his own life and space. The true unconditional unbounded love of GOD! The Universe coming through him. How shall he see it? How could he feel it? How would he know? What occurrences and events in his life, be they small or large, good or bad, affected and perhaps blocked his alignment with his true desire, to help make a difference on the planet.

To know, to see, hear, feel, and realize he was not sent here to be an average mortal. No, no, rather a spiritual being here on a mission.

Confused at times, occasionally distracted by worldly influences, he runs hard and fast on the chase; the chase for what -- more materials, more time? More freedom? Whose boundary conditions are driving his behaviors? Where do they come from?

So he would say, I, Kona, that very special Spirit in a dog form, changed everything and forever. I would say it was so much more than me! Do you understand who I really am?

● ● ● ●

(JOE)

I have been blessed through the stories and experiences of my life, to piece together a puzzle, to have ultimately attracted and manifested Kona to come and provide a daily consistent presence of love.

This has allowed me in many ways to want to be "Kona-like," to be simple at heart, full of love and passion, to laugh, to play, to walk in the woods, to climb the mountains, to just be for being's sake, to not worry about things I cannot control, to trust every day that God loves me, and through me loving me, and loving Kona, I love Him.

Go forward, attract your mirror; there is a "Kona" somewhere in your life, for your life. Receive your Kona. He is looking for you as well. Be open and focus on feeling great. Manifest it. Let it come to you. Remember mostly to live, laugh, love, and lighten up on you!

About the Author

Joe DeMartino is a native of New York city, married with two grown children and a grandson. He loves people, is an accomplished CEO, motivational speaker, personal trainer, marathoner and avid adventurer with a passion for hiking and climbing mountains.

Made in the USA
Middletown, DE
30 September 2020

20844548R00104